"Whether leading a US Army scout troop overseas or a non-profit here in the states, Charlie Hurdt strikes at the heart of what embodies high-performing organizations in his Team Leadership Handbook. This practical guide gives leaders a construct to think rightly about how to optimize performance and satisfaction and build a purpose-driven, disciplined team, with a culture of excellence. Every leader needs a model to anchor their leadership decisions and convey their approach. This work provides a brilliant start for any leader who desires a winning team."

- Major General Ed Thomas, USAF (Ret.)

I0539548

THE
Team Leadership
Handbook
EMPOWERING YOUR TEAM TO VICTORY

Charlie Hurdt

Preface

…There I was…embracing a memorable moment of excellence. Such a moment that my readers can assume the cost of such a sweet realization in one's life typically comes after much pain and toil and only happens on a rare special occasion. And on such an occasion, one tends to ponder all that has culminated leading to this moment and what all attributed to its success.

So, I enlighten my dear readers to this moment. There I was, 72 hours into a high-intensity and high-risk maneuver at the National Training Center. This period is notorious for failure, where sleep deprivation and a bold enemy counterattack can catastrophically annihilate our best intentions.

However, my company was determined and well-prepared for this. We developed contingencies for each probable failure and planned how to breach a heavily defended area and defend against an imminent counterattack. Sure 'enough, the enemy gained accurate reconnaissance from drones, planned timely artillery fire, positioned tanks to engage our narrow breach, jammed our satellite signal, struck with two attack helicopters, and held a tank and infantry company in reserve for a counterattack.

Despite the dire situation, we rehearsed and ensured perfect timing out of our "hide" positions, bypassed enemy artillery, screened our breach with effective counter-artillery against templated enemy tank positions, and engaged with our nine anti-tank guided missile (ATGM) Strykers while executing consecutive bounding movements. We seized the higher defensible terrain just in time to observe the incoming enemy counterattack of 10x tanks, 11x BMPs, and 2x attack helicopters (Hind-D). After the fight, we (simulated) lost 5x

ATGMs but had (simulated) destroyed 9x tanks, 10x BMPs, and 2x Hind-Ds.

We had our losses, but this was an incredible success. Our established and timely sustainment, the well orchestrated casualty evacuation, the exacting support from echeloned enablers, swift communication and reconsolidation, and our preparedness for yet another mission were executed beautifully and harmoniously. This was one of many training exercises and learning experiences we journeyed through, and I have to say- the first simulated exercises we practiced in early stages of training were quite the self reflective opposite of success. So, I reflected and asked, why? What made us victorious? Was it incredible superman leaders? Was it special super-soldiers?

No. We were average people, average leaders, and average soldiers. Dedicated to our profession and craft, yes, but no more than most in our field. Our level of camaraderie was exceptional, but so were other units. It was humbling yet encouraging as I pondered; we stood apart in success solely because of one outstanding factor- our team dynamic.

Our team dynamic was the advantage! We were fierce in our shared vision and purpose, our determination to ensure discipline, and our integral culture of trust and interdependence. Every single contingency became a realization, and we could have culminated at any point if it wasn't for someone else in our team adapting and supporting each other at every friction point.

From these experiences and historical studies, this handbook is born out of a deep-seated belief in the transformative power of team dynamics and the human dimension. Whereas, the best leaders are those who empower others to achieve greater things; and the best organizations are those that value and develop their people as essential members of their community.

These are the two underlying ideologies of *The Team Leadership Handbook*. That said, this handbook is *not* a leadership panacea. It is not built upon misguided individualistic philosophies such as "servant leadership," nor does it guarantee any altruistic, ethical, or moralistic agendas. Rather, this practical guide gives leaders a construct to think rightly about how to optimize performance and satisfaction and build a purpose-driven, disciplined team, with a culture of excellence.

Today's popular leadership philosophies, by and large, do not provide any concrete methods of how to operate within a complex team environment. Moreover, these modern philosophies are individualistic in their outlook. Certainly, if one desires personal development, they can practice any number of these individualist philosophies. They can demonstrate "servant leadership" or "transformational leadership" for all their worth. But at the end of the day, these leadership styles become a means to an end and a scheme for power. Even a "servant leader," by definition, embodies service as a means for increasing influential power, social praise, and their own self-esteem. So I became compelled to capture a team-oriented philosophy that I is derived from many enjoyed works, mentors, and influences.

While there are beneficial takeaways from these individualistic leadership philosophies, the common dynamic ultimately points to the legacy of "me," the social praise of "me," and the personal development of "me." Most leaders can attest, however, that leadership is not about the *leader*, it's about the *followers*. I emphasize "*followers*", because it implies those we are responsible to engage in positive influence, to include: peers, subordinates, superiors, and any relational interaction. Why, then, would we construct and commit to a leadership philosophy centered on the leader?

Leadership should be oriented around team dynamics.

There are many ways to develop team leadership skills, but leaders come in all shapes, sizes, backgrounds, and personalities. Hence, there is no "one-size-fits-all" approach to leadership. Institutions have taught various leadership styles – Transformational, Transactional, Servant-Leader, Authentic, Autocratic, and Democratic – as popular means to cultivate future leaders. However, the most applicable and discernible approaches I have enjoyed in a team dynamic are the Adaptive Leadership Theory and the Situational Leadership Model.

Certainly, there are profound aspects to learn from each of these leadership styles. Yet, no organization, whether public or private, holistically embodies or even agrees upon any one of these leadership philosophies. While they encourage their leaders to seek personal growth and leadership maturity, these organizations have never operated simply as a group of leaders but rather as a network of teams. The greater issue arises when a positional leader adopts an individual philosophy and expects everyone else to adapt without offering the same consideration.

As such, this handbook introduces a framework and philosophy for *team-oriented leadership*, a dynamic leadership style that prioritizes, facilitates, and optimizes teamwork. Several noteworthy books and courses have been written for developing teamwork. Yet there stands no leadership philosophy to unite and define those beliefs…until now.

I deeply value clear insights into team dynamics and the human dimension. Inspired by the *five love languages*, which have permeated our modern society to foster greater empathy and appreciation for personality differences, I recognized an opportunity to enhance the team leadership handbook. By incorporating *seven leader archetypes*, we can offer a profound understanding and appreciation of the diverse work styles and relational aptitudes that align with the personalities of various team roles. This approach not only enhances team synergy, but also fosters a more inclusive and empathetic work environment, where each leader's unique contributions are recognized and valued.

The Team Leadership Handbook, therefore, is the definitive guide for implementing team-oriented leadership. Drawing from numerous works and other leadership and management systems, *The Team Leadership Handbook* has taken few yet meaningful references, and refined them into a measured, easy-to-use framework primed for any team endeavor. This handbook will allow scholars to build upon a common foundation, and provide institutions with a pathway to develop their team leaders and synergize team collaborations across any environment.

Table of Contents

Table of Contents

Introduction

In the ever-evolving landscape of modern organizations, the essence of success lies not in individual brilliance but in the collective synergy of a well-coordinated team. The "Team Leadership Handbook" is a comprehensive guide designed to equip leaders with the tools, philosophies, and strategies needed to cultivate high-performing teams that thrive in the face of adversity and scarcity.

Drawing inspiration from diverse fields such as military strategy, business management, and psychology, this handbook delves into the principles of team leadership, collaboration, and innovation. It offers a structured framework that empowers leaders to navigate the complexities of team dynamics, foster a culture of mutual respect and purpose, and drive their teams towards exceptional performance and satisfaction.

Throughout this handbook, you will discover practical insights and actionable strategies that have been refined through years of experience and research. From understanding the foundational principles of team culture, purpose, and discipline, to mastering the art of collaboration through the Six Steps of Team Collaboration (TCP), this book provides a roadmap for leaders to build cohesive, resilient, and adaptive teams.

As you embark on this journey, you will be introduced to the key archetypes that define successful teams, each bringing unique strengths and perspectives to the table. Whether you are a seasoned leader or a new team member, the "Team Leadership Handbook" will serve as your trusted companion, guiding you through the challenges and opportunities of team leadership.

Prepare to unlock the full potential of your team, harness the power of collaboration, and achieve remarkable results. Welcome to the "Team Leadership Handbook," where the journey to team excellence begins.

> *"Being a leader is not about you. It's about the people that are on your team and how you can help them be successful."*
>
> — *Susan Vobejda*
>
> *"The way a team plays as a whole determines its success. You may have the greatest bunch of individual stars in the world, but if they don't play together, the club won't be worth a dime."*
>
> — *Babe Ruth*

Chapter 1:
The Realm of Scarcity and Adversity

The realm in which we operate is full of scarcity and adversity. For any leader, effective planning and decision making begins with understanding your environmental context and maintaining situational awareness. As a leader, your situational awareness should be predicated on the ideas of *scarcity* and *adversity*. These two qualities will allow you, the leader, to identify your team's strengths and weaknesses, and position the team members accordingly.

Well-performing teams are vital to the success of any organization. Some organizations, such as the US military, specialize in training teams that perform under conditions of scarcity and adversity. Many businesses are composed of intra-cooperative teams – Human Resources, Accounting, Distribution, Public Affairs, etc. – because their specialized tasks can only be accomplished through the synchronized effort of a specialized team. Thus, if any organization wishes to formulate and teach a collaborative process or leadership style, they must first address the environmental barriers of scarcity and adversity.

Scarcity

Whether addressing military, political, or economic circumstances, *scarcity* will always be the common denominator. In fact, scarcity is the very reason why economics and war exist. Resources are always limited; therefore, efficiency through collaboration is imperative. Performance achieves its full potential through synergy, where each person performs better as a member of the team than they could perform individually. General Stanley McChrystal, who rose to prominence as the commander of the International Security Assistance Force (Afghanistan) and the US Joint Special Operations Command, wrote his book *Team of Teams* as a blueprint for how humans should work together. When people work together as a highly-communicative "team of teams," it creates superior awareness, assessment, and adaptive creativity in a time-constrained environment.

Understandably, everything we do as humans, individually and collectively, turns out to be "time-constrained." Thus, *time* is the most critical element of scarcity.

Indeed, time is the one resource that we can never replenish. Therefore, a good rule of thumb for establishing your team's timetable is the *One-Third, Two-Thirds Rule*. This rule states that leaders should use *one-third* of their allocated time for planning, while giving their subordinates the remaining *two-thirds* of the available time for planning and preparation at their own level. In other words, when a team is given a task to perform (with a stated deadline), the leader should compute the total time available for his team to complete the task. The team leader should then allow himself no more than one-third of the available time to complete his plan, while allocating the other two-thirds to the people he leads.

Following the One-Third, Two-Thirds Rule involves constant communication and feedback among team members. It also involves empowering your subordinates to plan at their level. One of the best ways, therefore, to facilitate this empowerment and feedback loop is to share information with your team members as soon as possible. Stove-piping and withholding information (unless there is a security risk) will hamstring the productivity within your team. This is especially true in cases of unfavorable information, wherein your team may have to shift its priorities or pivot onto a new course. There's an old adage that states: "Bad news doesn't get better with time." Share information early and share it often. In the end, it will be one of the best ways to manage the scarcity of time.

In the United States Army, for example, units relay and disseminate information via the formal "orders" process. This three-tier system, although more formal and rigid than most organizations, can be applied to nearly any business or civilian organization.

1) **Warning Order:** An informal "heads-up" to the applicable team members. The Warning Order contains the 5 W's (Who, What, Where, When, Why) and will likely include key events along with an estimated timeline for completion. The Warning Order is critical for facilitating time management among subordinates, and will give them a general idea of what their team needs to accomplish as part of the bigger task.

2) **Operations Order:** The Operations Order is a more-detailed plan, assigning key tasks to subordinates, and outlining the standards for execution. In a pure military context, it also describes the enemy situation, anticipated threats, and what supportive elements will be present throughout the operation. The Operations Order will allow your team members to narrow their focus (and refine their tasks, if needed) to complete the team's mission.

3) **Fragmentary Order:** After the Operations Order has been shared, the "Fragmentary Order" announces any changes or revisions to the existing plan. These changes could be situational ("Our deadline has been moved back by six weeks.") or incidental ("The price of this commodity has dropped during the past week. Please adjust your team's budget accordingly."). Regardless, the disseminated information must be specific and directed towards those affected by the change.

But mitigating temporal scarcity is only part of the battle. A leader, via his collaborative process, must be able to identify all areas of scarcity, and develop appropriate courses of action. Each manifestation of scarcity will impact how your team approaches their mission and how they allocate their resources. Scarcity may take many forms but, for the purposes of this handbook, we will focus on four established types:

1) Incidental Scarcity
2) Conditional Scarcity
3) Episodic Scarcity
4) Chronic Scarcity

Incidental Scarcity: Typically, these are low-intensity, short-term disruptions. Generally speaking, teams can still perform their essential functions even if they encounter an occasional bout of incidental scarcity. For example, a business may use alternative brands or purchase from a different vendor due to supply-chain issues.

A real-life example of mitigating Incidental Scarcity occurred in May 2020. During the COVID-19 pandemic (and the onset of the "Great Resignation"), Primary Kids Inc, an online retailer of children's clothing, took a novel approach to preventing the loss of its workforce. Indeed, the company instituted a 4-day work week. As a result, Primary Kids boasted a retention rate of 93% while other companies were bleeding personnel at an alarming rate.

Conditional Scarcity: Much like Incidental Scarcity, Conditional Scarcity is low-intensity, but longer in duration. When a team experiences Conditional Scarcity, they must develop long-term compensatory strategies. This could include restructuring budgets, consolidating teams, workspace downsizing, repurposing tools and resources, etc.

Patagonia, the famed outdoor clothing company, developed a unique approach to mitigating Conditional Scarcity. As part of its company policy, Patagonia provides maternity leave and onsite daycare. This people-oriented approach solved the problem of Conditional Scarcity while maintaining high morale in the workplace. Over the ensuing five years, Patagonia retained 100% of their female employees who took maternity leave – significantly higher than the US average of 79%.

Episodic Scarcity: A high-intensity, but intermittent, form of scarcity. In the business world, episodic scarcity will likely follow periods of economic boom and bust. Macro-level examples include the Great Depression (1929-1941) and the Great Recession (2007-09). Micro-level examples include realtors who compensate for a drop in homebuyers or the automotive industry accepting government "bailouts" in the face of falling profits.

Sometimes, Episodic Scarcity can lead to innovations that benefit both the business and the consumer. The tradeoff, however, is that the business typically incurs a short-term loss. Well Fargo, for example, unveiled a "customer relief program" in the wake of Hurricane Harvey and the California wildfires. These benefits included a suspension of late fees; freezing credit reports; deferring mortgage payments; and loan modifications. Although Wells Fargo took a short-term loss in fee revenue, these compassionate policies had a tremendous downstream effect. Respectively, customers received short-term and long-term relief in the form of: (a) reduced financial burdens, and (b) the opportunity to remain solvent while rebuilding their lives in the wake of a natural disaster. This, in turn, led to a reduced default rate, saving Wells Fargo more money in the long term. Additionally, Wells Fargo's reputation soared, which led to a dramatic increase in customer referrals and new account holders.

Chronic Scarcity: This is the most severe form of scarcity. Long-term and high-intensity, this brand of scarcity prevents teams from achieving their goals. Whenever a team encounters Chronic Scarcity, they are typically on the verge of obsolescence. Either: (a) their products and services are no longer relevant to the market, or (b) the team's purpose no longer aligns with the goals of its parent organization. For example, following the end of the Cold War, the US Army's contingent in Western Europe shrunk to nearly half of what it had been during the early 1980s. Now that the Soviet Union had dissolved (and the Iron Curtain had fallen) American troops were no longer essential to the security of mainland Europe. Chronic Scarcity, however, is not necessarily a death sentence. Survival often comes in the form of aggressive rebranding and/or restructuring.

The Chrysler Corporation was a latter-day "case study" of an organization that bounced back from the abyss of Chronic Scarcity. By the late 1970s, Chrysler was on the verge of collapse. Already the smallest of the "Big Three" automakers, Chrysler and its marques were struggling to compete with GM, Ford, and the growing incursion of Japanese automakers. The quality of their cars had fallen drastically over the decade, which led to a scarcity of buyers *and* credibility. Enter Lee Iacocca: the man whose aggressive restructuring saved Chrysler from liquidation, and turned the automaker into a powerhouse of the 1980s.

Adversity

Alongside scarcity, *adversity* is always present. In order to lead your team through adversity, however, you must first identify your "enemy." Practically speaking, the enemy could be a toxic leader, poor work satisfaction, fierce market competition, a workplace rivalry, or a financial crisis. In short, the enemy is an opponent that one must face when striving to achieve certain goals. Thus, it is vital for teams to identify their "enemy," both metaphorically and practically.

However, finding and confronting these enemies is not a bad thing. Before confronting the enemy, however, your team must coalesce around a shared vision and hope. Whatever that shared vision may be, it must be clearly-defined and agreed upon by the team members.

History is replete with examples of businesses and organizations that stood strong in the face of adversity; clearly defined their "enemy;" and formulated a plan to take the enemy down. For instance, by 1997, the once-mighty Apple Computers was the "sick man of Silicon Valley." Following Steve Jobs' exile in 1985, Apple lost more of its market share every year while the company fumbled to find a strategic direction. Meanwhile, Microsoft, IBM, and the ever-growing stable of PCs began dominating the market. Amidst these trends, Apple posted a $1 billion loss for 1996-97 and laid off a third of the workforce. Their unwieldy product line included dozens obsolete and redundant items. If these trends continued, the company would go bankrupt within 90 days.

When Steve Jobs returned to Apple, he quickly identified the "enemies" as: (a) poor product management, and (b) the zero-sum game mentality. Retaking the reins, Jobs cut 70% of Apple's product line. He then stunned the world by announcing a partnership with Microsoft. Indeed, his former rival would invest $150 million into Apple; in turn, Apple's operating system would support Microsoft Office on the new iMac. As Jobs explained: "If we want to move forward and see Apple healthy and prospering again, we have to let go of a few things here. We have to let go of this notion that for Apple to win, Microsoft has to lose."

Within one year, Steve Jobs turned Apple's $1 billion loss into a $300 million profit. Almost simultaneously, he launched the "Think Different" campaign, highlighting the iMac G3, the ubiquitous brightly-colored, all-in-one desktop. By the end of the early 2000s, the iPod and iPhone had reestablished Apple as a global tech powerhouse. By 2018, it was the first publicly-traded American company with a trillion-dollar value.

The following chapters define and describe the doctrinal characteristics of the Team Collaboration Process within the Realm of Scarcity and Adversity. These chapters also provide a detailed discussion of each pillar within the Team Collaboration Process. The reader will also learn how to guide the Team Collaboration Process in a time-constrained environment. Effectively conducting this process, however, requires *each* team member to embody these fundamentals of collaboration.

As seen in the following pictogram (Figure 1), the Realm of Scarcity and Adversity is always present. It is akin to a dense fog through which your team can learn to maneuver. The cluster of dots represent different individuals who can merge into an effective team if they have purpose, discipline, and culture.

- **Purpose** gives every member meaning and direction, but also a sense of identity towards the group.
- **Culture** increases the unity and cohesion of the group to form a stronger team bond.
- **Discipline** is what maintains good order and boundaries for the team, but also focuses effort, increases efficiency, and strengthens the team's capabilities.

When the team coalesces around the shared concepts of purpose, culture, and discipline, they can rapidly adapt and maneuver effectively through the fog of Scarcity and Adversity.

Figure 1: Journey Through the Realm of Scarcity and Adversity

Team Leadership
Conceptual Model

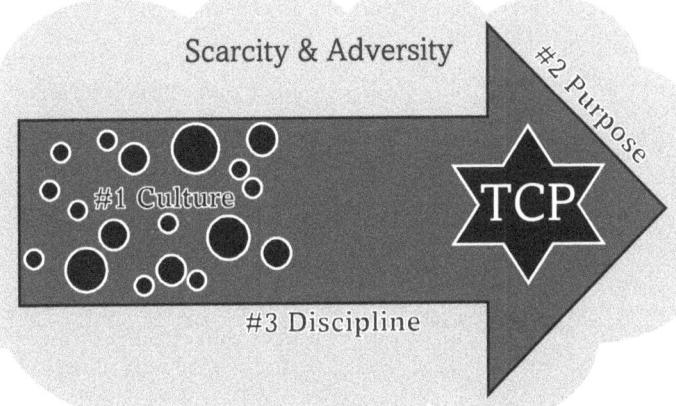

Scarcity & Adversity

#1 Culture

#2 Purpose

TCP

#3 Discipline

Team Leadership Philosophy:		Team Collaboration Process:
3 Principles that Merge Individuals into a Team and Lead Them through the Fog		Creates a Dynamic Synergy Process that Drives Momentum and Maneuver

Relationship that chaos, when orchestrated, produces a magnificent symphony of individual talents and capabilities. Unified chaos in diversity, skills, experience produce unique and remarkable results that are highly adaptable, unpredictable, and cultivate harmonical success that would be unrealized with a divided approach.

Chapter 2:
Team Leadership Philosophy

The Team Leadership Philosophy is designed to form an interdependent-function of leadership instead of an autocratic/hierarchal form of leadership. Too often, individual leaders are scapegoated for a team's failure, or praised for its success. Although positional leaders are responsible for their team's action or inaction, we must not discount the influential value and responsibility of every team member. In fact, leaders should not be the single point of failure for any operation; rather, they should be surrounded by an adequate team.

By definition, a leader provides guidance and is accountable for authoritative decisions. Therefore, the Team Leadership Philosophy characterizes the leader as a proverbial "gardener" – cultivating the ideal environment for team collaboration. The team leader assumes three responsibilities as the foundation upon which to build this environment:

1) Create culture
2) Provide purpose
3) Ensure discipline

Conceptual Framework

Team leadership is a critical concept for any organization that wants to be successful. In this conceptual framework, we will explore the idea of team leadership, drawing on the example of the Special Forces Operational Detachment Alpha (ODA). The ODA is a highly effective team that achieve its goals through a combination of individual expertise, cross-training, and a strong sense of shared purpose.

We will begin by discussing the importance of team leadership in today's organizations. Then, we will explore the key elements of team leadership, including: *Shared Purpose; Individual Expertise; Cross-Training; Strong Communication;* and *Trust.*

Shared purpose: Both ODAs and business organizations have a shared purpose. For ODAs, this is to achieve military objectives through intensive training. For business organizations, this is to make a profit through an excellent product and service.

Individual expertise: Both ODAs and business organizations are made up of individuals with unique expertise. For ODAs, this includes expertise in areas such as high-risk operations, intelligence, and logistics. For business organizations, this includes expertise in areas such as marketing, finance, and low-risk operations.

Cross-training: Both ODAs and business organizations encourage cross-training. This allows team members to fill in for each other when needed and to develop a deeper understanding of the organization's overall goals.

Strong communication: Both ODAs and business organizations require strong communication. This allows team members to share information, coordinate their efforts, and make decisions quickly and effectively.

Trust: Both ODAs and business organizations require trust. This allows team members to rely on each other and to work together effectively.

In addition to these similarities, there are also some parallels between ODAs and business organizations. Both ODAs and business organizations are subject to change. In the military, this change can be brought about by new missions, new tactics and assets, or new threats. In the business world, this change can be brought about by new market conditions, new competitors, or new technologies. Both ODAs and business organizations are subject to rules and regulations. These rules and regulations are designed to ensure that both organizations operate in a safe, legally sound, and ethical manner. By complying with these rules and regulations, ODAs and business organizations can help to ensure the safety of their personnel, protection of the public, and the integrity of their organizations.

We will then conclude by discussing the benefits of team leadership. Team leadership can lead to increased productivity, improved morale, and enhanced creativity. Finally, we encourage you to apply these principles to your own organization in order to improve its performance.

The Special Forces Operational Detachment Alpha (ODA) is also known as the "A-Team." It is one of the most recognizable examples of team leadership, exemplified in one of the world's most elite forces, conducting high-risk, time-constrained operations. These teams have designed their task organization around the specialized purpose of their missions.

ODA teams do not hire individuals. **They hire teammates for specific roles.**

This approach to team building is based on the principle of complementary expertise. Each ODA team member has a unique set of skills and experience that they bring to the team. This allows the team to achieve its goals more effectively than if it were made up of individuals with the same skills and experience.

The ODA team structure is also designed to promote interdependence. Team members are not expected to be experts in all areas. Instead, they are expected to be able to work effectively with others to achieve the team's goals. This interdependence helps to create a strong, cohesive team that can overcome any challenge.

The ODA team structure is a proven model for success. It has been used by Special Forces to achieve some of the most difficult missions in the world. This model can be applied to any team, regardless of the industry or field of work. By hiring teammmates for specific roles and promoting interdependence, teams can achieve their goals more effectively and efficiently.

There are five A-Teams per Company, known as "B-teams," and there are three B-teams in each Special Forces Battalion, "C-Team." Then there are three C-Teams in a Special Forces Group. It is designed to be a network of teams; each possessing unique capabilities and focuses that empower an interdependent autonomy.

Each ODA is made up of 12 men, each with a separate Military Occupational Specialty (MOS) while also cross-trained in other specialties. A typical 12-man ODA comprises:

1) 1x Detachment Commander
2) 1x Assistant Detachment Commander
3) 1x Operations Sergeant
4) 1x Assistant Operations and Intelligence Sergeant
5) 2x Weapons Sergeants
6) 2x Communications Sergeants
7) 2x Medical Sergeants
8) 2x Engineering Sergeants

The Detachment Commander is referred to and known as the Team Leader. It is the Team Leader's responsibility to outfit his team, organize and brief missions, and coordinate mission objectives with B-Team. Essentially, the Team Leader is accountable for risk mitigation, decision-making, and facilitation. The effectiveness of the Team Leader is measured by the culture climate, communicating purpose, and ensuring discipline.

As mentioned, each member is cross-trained, and many responsibilities overlap or are redundant for the sake of strengthening the chain of responsibilities and protecting the ability to complete missions. For example, the Assistant Detachment Commander assumes the Team Leader role if needed, and the Operations Sergeant is responsible for the overall organization, functionality and training the 'A-Team' while also ensuring sure the team is outfitted correctly and supports the Team Leader. Each team member is linked into the chain of responsibility and is ready to assume primary, alternate, contingent, or emergency responsibilities when required. The interdependent chain of responsibility creates a dynamic team that is adept to tenaciously fight and adapt until the last man standing.

Too often, managerial departments – including finance, human resources, marketing, and even administration – will act as individual entities. They plan inside their own vacuum, causing desynchronization and miscommunication within the organization. Examples are so numerous that many organizations have accepted this cognitive dissonance as normal.

Team leadership can help organizations overcome these challenges by creating a shared mindset and encouraging cross-communication. When team leaders create a culture of collaboration, it allows individuals and departments to share expertise and work together towards common goals. This can lead to increased innovation, productivity, and efficiency.

For example, a team leader can encourage cross-communication between the finance and marketing departments. This can help the two departments better understand each other's needs and priorities. As a result, they can work together to develop more effective marketing campaigns that are aligned with the company's financial goals.

> *"Team leadership will equip organizations to break-through the challenges of siloed departments and ineffective communication."*
>
> *— Charlie Hurdt*

Team leadership can also help organizations to achieve nested and complimentary goals. When team members have a shared understanding of the organization's overall goals, they are more likely to work together in a way that supports those goals.

Overall, team leadership is a powerful tool that can help organizations to overcome the challenges of siloed departments and ineffective communication. By creating a shared mindset and encouraging cross-communication, team leaders can help their organizations to achieve their goals more effectively and efficiently.

Defining Team Leadership with a KISS

Names have meaning. Team Leadership is a name that should not be misunderstood or morphed into other ideas. The saying, "Keep it simple, stupid" (KISS) is the integral idea of team leadership, and reminds readers that acronyms carry power, and that simplicity enables understanding and application. And so, using the same acronym, we can define Team Leadership with a KISS.

Keen, Initiative, Steward, Synergy (KISS) is a mindset that can be adopted by anyone, regardless of their role or position. It emphasizes the importance of being proactive, taking responsibility, and working together to achieve common goals.

K: Keen individuals are always looking for discernment in how things ought to be done. They continuously seek out information, ideas, and mentorship; they establish confidence to take calculated risks. They search for insight on their own performance, as well as the performance of their team or whatever organization to which they belong.

I: Initiative is the ability to take action without being asked. Initiating individuals are not afraid to step up and take charge.

They drive against the impulse of complacency, lackluster performance, and stale creativity. They understand that taking initiative is a mindset that shapes an organization's outcomes.

S: Stewardship is the act of taking care of something. In the context of KISS, stewardship refers to taking care of the team's resources, both human and material. Stewards remain mindful of the resources they have at their disposal. They make sure to use them wisely and efficiently.

S: Synergy is the cooperation of two or more agents or forces so that their combined effect is greater than the sum of their individual parts. In the context of KISS, synergy refers to a team working together to achieve more than they could individually. Keen individuals create a culture of collaboration and cooperation, and they encourage team members to share their ideas and expertise. They are always looking for ways to leverage the strengths of each team member and to create a team that is greater than the sum of its parts.

KISS is a mindset and profession that can help individuals and teams achieve great things. When individuals are keen, take initiative, steward resources wisely, and create synergy, they can create a number of positive outcomes, including: increased productivity, improved morale, and enhanced creativity.

K *een*

I *nitiative*

S *tewarding*

S *ynergy*

The KISS mindset creates team camaraderie and drives innovation. But even the most cohesive and mutually-supportive team can fall short of its goals if it's not properly led. In the next chapter, we will explore the three operating principles of team leadership, and how these principles (working in conjunction with the KISS mentality) can enable your team to achieve new levels of productivity with an unparalleled workplace dynamism.

Figure 2: Team Leadership Conceptual Model

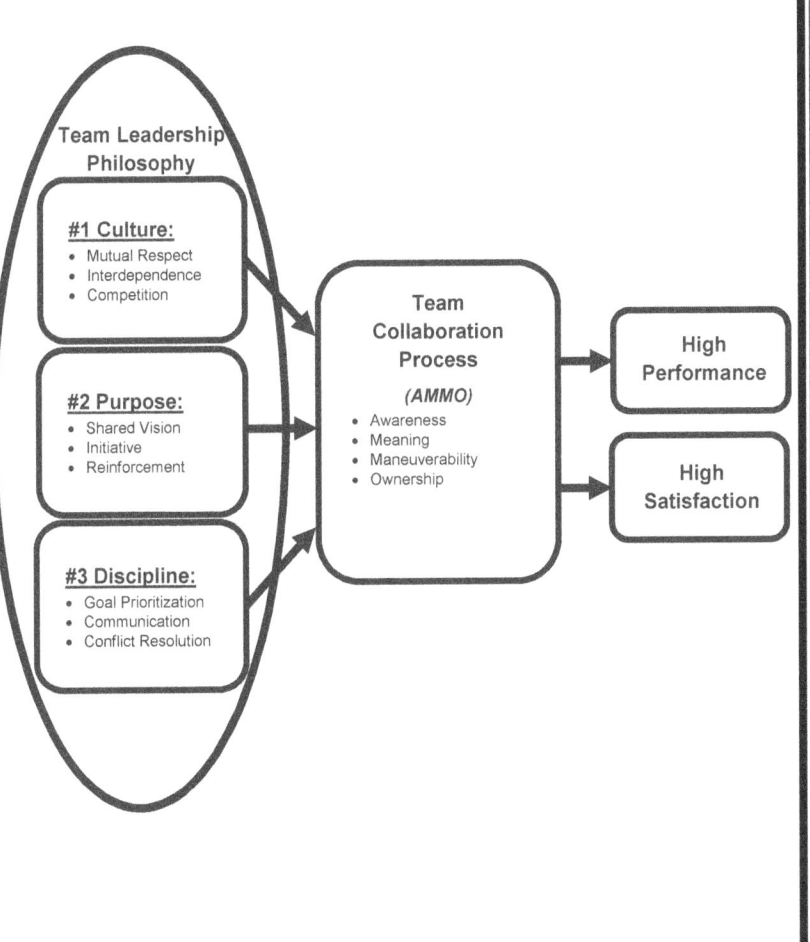

Chapter 3:
The Three Principles of
Team Leadership

The entire building collapses without a solid foundation. In today's competitive business world, it is more important than ever for teams to have common doctrines upon which they can build that foundation. But what makes a superlative team? We will explore three principles of team leadership: *culture*, *purpose*, and *discipline*.

Culture: Cultivating a unique culture is the essence of any successful team. As a leader, you must understand and steward your team's culture. Team cultures must be adaptable to external forces, but they can be extremely fragile when toxic behaviors erupt from within. Thus, a well-stewarded culture will thrive with encouraged, motivated team members.

Purpose: Purpose is the driving force behind a team's existence. A clearly defined and shared purpose aligns the team's effort towards a common objective. It instills a sense of meaning; and it empowers individuals to recognize the value of their contributions. When team members understand the "why" behind their work, they exhibit heightened engagement, productivity, and commitment.

Discipline: Discipline is critical for team success. It promotes order, accountability, and productivity. Disciplined team members adhere to established rules, enabling effective workflow across the organization. They are focused, organized, and committed, taking ownership of their work. This, in turn, fosters a climate of trust and respect. Discipline minimizes conflicts, encourages open communication, and creates a harmonious work environment. Additionally, it helps team members develop qualities like self-control and resilience, contributing to their personal and professional growth. A team that fails to value discipline will inevitably devolve into chaos.

Maintaining team discipline, therefore, begins with these three tenets: *goal prioritization*, *communication*, and *conflict resolution*.

Any team that lacks a strong foundation (built upon culture, purpose, and discipline) cannot achieve sustained success. For the purposes of this handbook, we define "success" as: (a) the team's overall performance in accomplishing their mission; and (b) job satisfaction amongst the individual team members.

Culture fosters mutual respect, interdependence, and healthy competition, creating a vibrant and resilient team spirit. Purpose unites team members with a shared vision, driving engagement and productivity. Discipline ensures order, accountability, and effective conflict resolution, thereby facilitating a high-performance team environment. By understanding and embodying these key principles, team leaders can cultivate exceptional teams capable of achieving remarkable results.

#1 Culture

As mentioned above, the three aspects of a team culture are composed of mutual respect, interdependence, and healthy competition. When these three aspects are habitually incorporated, it enables discernment, empathy, and tact. Culture is the foremost principle that will make or break an organization because it directly appeals to intrinsic motivation, which is the very essence of work satisfaction.

1) **Mutual Respect:** Foster dignity and respect; fiercely protect our integrity and trust; and do not tolerate complacent misconduct. The most practical applications for

cultivating mutual respect are often simple acts of kindness. The most common (and most appreciated) practices are 1) spending attentive time, 2) creating meaningful dialogue, and 3) recognizing another's labor, effort, and development.

2) **Interdependence:** Uphold a transformational learning environment where each person holds significant value in a cohesive, interdependent team.

3) **Competition:** Unrelenting and passionate; seek out and destroy the enemy. Also, remain vigilant against corruption from within.

Also, when establishing an organizational culture, develop a phrase or slogan that reflects the organization's mission (for example: "Just Do It;" "Quality never goes out of style;" "If you can find a better car, buy it."). Slogans like these can be used as closing remarks for team meetings or other events. Make your team members repeat this slogan on a regular basis, even beyond the point where they make fun of it, because by then the philosophy will be fully ingrained in the mindset of every member.

#2 Purpose

A team's purpose is its reason for being. It is what drives the team to work together and achieve its goals. A clear and shared purpose helps to unify team members and focus their efforts on a common goal. When team members know why they are working together, they are more likely to be engaged and productive. The three fundamental aspects to a team's purpose are *shared vision*, *initiative*, and *reinforcement*.

1) **Shared vision:** A shared vision is a common understanding of what the team is trying to achieve. It is

important for team members to have a shared vision because it gives them a sense of purpose and direction.

2) **Initiative:** Initiative is the willingness to take action and solve problems. A team that is full of initiative is a team that is constantly moving forward and making progress. When team members are willing to take ownership of their work and solve problems, they are more likely to be successful.

However, the leader must ensure that his team members learn to take "disciplined initiative." Disciplined initiative means not making hasty decisions or taking initiative simply for its own sake. Rather, disciplined initiative means knowing the organization's culture, and using that knowledge to anticipate future needs and make independent decisions conducive to the organization's goals. Disciplined initiative does not appear on its own; the leader must cultivate it within the team.

3) **Reinforcement:** Reinforcement is the act of rewarding positive behaviors and incremental achievements. Reinforcement helps team members stay motivated and engaged. When team members know that their efforts are appreciated, they are more likely to continue working hard.

A team with a clear and shared purpose, initiative, and reinforcement is a team that is more likely to be successful. By following these three principles, team leaders can develop teams that are productive, motivated, and successful.

Here are some additional tips for developing a strong team purpose:

- Involve team members in the process of creating the purpose. This will help to ensure that the purpose is something that everyone's committed to.

- Make the purpose **S.M.A.R.T** - *Specific, Measurable, Achievable, Relevant,* and *Time bound.* This will ensure that the purpose is something that can the team can achieve.
- Communicate the purpose to team members regularly. This will help to keep everyone focused and motivated.
- Celebrate successes along the way. This will help to reinforce the purpose and keep team members motivated.

By fostering a shared vision, cultivating disciplined initiative, and providing consistent reinforcement, leaders can build teams that are intrinsically motivated. A strong team purpose is not a static goal but an evolving journey, requiring continuous communication, adaptation, and celebration of milestones. Through these concerted efforts, teams can achieve remarkable results while fostering a sense of fulfillment and shared accomplishment.

#3 Discipline

Discipline is essential for any team that wants to function effectively and efficiently. It helps to ensure that team members are focused on their goals, that they communicate effectively, and that they are able to resolve conflicts in a productive way. The three aspects of team discipline are *goal prioritization, communication,* and *conflict resolution.*

1) **Goal Prioritization:** Focus the team's resources and efforts on the primary objective. Prioritizing goals is the process of ranking them based on their urgency. It helps the team focus on their most critical tasks and avoids getting them bogged down on less important matters. As a leader, it can be hard to track your team's progress if they don't have a set of priority tasks.

One method to prioritize goals is to create a **goal hierarchy.** This hierarchy can take on almost any format, as long as it sequentially ranks the goals in order of importance. One popular example of a goal hierarchy is the Eisenhower Matrix (Figure 3). This tool categorizes goals into different quadrants based on their relative urgency and importance.

FIGURE 3: THE EISENHOWER MATRIX

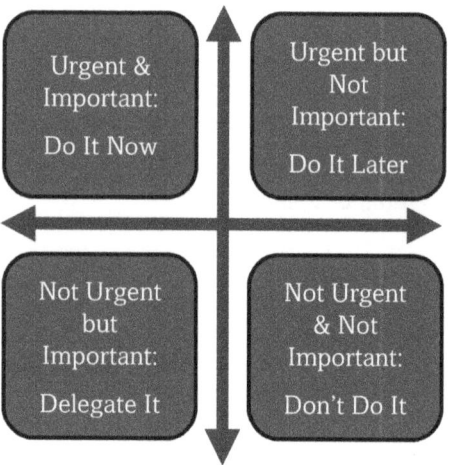

Aside from the SMART acronym discussed in the "Purpose" section, another acronym to facilitate goal prioritization is **W.O.O.P** – *Wish, Outcome, Obstacle,* and *Plan.* First, state what you wish to achieve. Then, envision the outcome and how you want your team to feel once they've achieved that goal. Next, identify any known or potential obstacles and start developing plans to overcome them. Finally, organize the plan and ensure that the planning process is a collaborative effort. Under this construct, it will be easier to identify any potential issues that could prevent the team from reaching its desired goals.

2) **Communication:** Using clear and effective communication is vital for establishing a culture of competence, truth, and vigilance. In the realm of team leadership, *tact* is bedrock of effective communication. Interpersonal tact is essential to building a collaborative environment. Tact will intrinsically inspire purpose and/or creativity within the team, rather than having them rely on extrinsic pressures.

3) **Conflict Resolution:** It's fascinating to explore the different ways in which a leader can resolve conflict. There are five commonly-known styles of conflict management: Accommodate; Avoid; Compromise; Compete; and Collaborate. A team leader needs to facilitate *each* of these five styles in order to maintain an effective team. By its very nature, a team should *accommodate* each other's values and expertise, *avoid* conflicts that are unnecessary or non-beneficial, jointly *compete* against competitors and adversaries, *compromise* into a shared vision and goals, and *collaborate* towards the accomplishment of those goals. (Song et al, 2006). But the five conflict management styles are only part of the equation. Successful conflict resolution is measured by: a) the swift administration of justice against misbehavior, and b) setting the conditions necessary to minimize the likelihood of recurrence.

The So What

The three principles of team leadership – culture, purpose, and discipline – are interrelated. A strong team culture is essential for creating a team with a clear purpose. And a disciplined team is more likely to be successful when it is built upon a foundation of mutual respect, interdependence, and competition.

A team with a strong culture is one where team members feel valued and respected. They feel like they are part of something bigger than themselves. They are motivated to work hard and achieve their goals.

Why building the team culture matters and organizations must invest and prioritize time for extracurricular social events:

- Team members feel valued, respected, and supported.
- They are motivated to work hard and achieve the team's goals.
- They are more likely to stay with the team for the long term.
- They are more likely to be productive and efficient.
- They are more likely to be creative and innovative.

A team with a clear purpose is one that knows what it is working towards. They have a shared vision for the future.

Why themes and messaging matter in daily, weekly, monthly, and annual meetings:

- Team members have a sense of direction and focus.
- They are more likely to be successful because they know what they are working towards.
- They are more likely to be motivated and engaged.
- They are more likely to be creative and innovative.

A disciplined team is one that is organized and efficient. They know how to prioritize their work and they are able to get things done. They are also able to resolve conflict effectively.

Why performance training and hardships are critical to resilient discipline:

- Team members are organized and efficient.
- They know how to work together, and they are able to get things done.
- They are also able to resolve conflict effectively.
- Standards are identified and enforced
- Nurtures trust and appreciative understanding for decisions and outcomes.

The three principles of team leadership are not always easy to implement. It takes time, effort, and commitment to create a strong, successful team. But the rewards are worth it. A strong team can achieve great things. If you are a team leader, I encourage you to focus on these three principles. By doing so, you can create a team that is capable of achieving anything.

Imagine a team that is so passionate about its work that they can't wait to get started each day; a team that is so focused on its goals that they're willing to put in the extra effort to achieve them; managing their time for off-the-clock recovery and on-the-clock work ethic. A team that is so supportive of each other that they are always willing to help each other out. This is the kind of team that can achieve anything.

Figure 4: Three Pillars of Team Leadership

Chapter 4:
Team Collaboration Process

The Team Collaboration Process (TCP) is all about the mastery of fundamentals. It draws upon several planning ideologies – in particular, the Military Decision-Making Process (MDMP). MDMP is remarkably effective in both war and peacetime. More importantly, however, MDMP is synergetic among even the most diverse groups because each member must be *interdependent*, regardless of rank or individual differences.

The phrases "team leadership" and "team collaboration" imply that each member is empowered to act with the leader's intent. This spirit of interdependence yields the best possible team performance, and reciprocally empowers the team leader to make effective decisions and give proper guidance. Stifling this interdependence leads to indecisiveness, frustration, and unnecessary divisions within the team.

TCP is a unifying approach wherein each member is accountable to seize the initiative and share insight because of their inherent responsibility to the team. The goal of TCP is to formulate a fundamental process for strategizing a unified effort within a time-constrained, adversarial environment.

TCP, supported by the Team Leadership Philosophy discussed in Chapter 2, is designed to create a holistic approach to successfully maneuver your team in a competitive environment.

Conceptual Framework

Imagine that there is a divisional leader who is tasked to recommend budget cuts, optimize production costs, and develop a new marketing strategy.

- Should he use a transformational leadership approach to obtain individual buy-in and insight so that he can be more discerning?
- Should he adopt a servant-leader mentality? – prioritizing "people-first, mission always" yet not gaining the practical knowledge needed to make an effective decision?
- How about being authentic to his own individual reasoning and efforts? Will that be enough to ease the conscious weight of shutting down a department?

Sometimes, leaders wrestle with intrusive memories of *"What if I could do it all over again?"* That's often because they relied too much on their own individual assessment when making decisions.

This handbook argues that individual efforts are wholly inadequate for realizing complex and innovative solutions, no matter how much knowledge or individual expertise a leader may have. It is only when a team's synergetic effort comes together that blind spots are revealed and unique perspectives (with shared expertise) yield groundbreaking ideas. Wielding the Team Leadership Philosophy, combined with the Team Collaboration Process, produces an inspiring momentum to extrapolate the best course of action while giving the utmost confidence and resting satisfaction…no matter the results.

Defining the Team Collaboration Process

Whereas "Team Collaboration" is straightforward, the "Process" is not. It's not just a planning process; it's also a social process. The desired outcomes are efficiency and excellence. But can creating an elaborate process guarantee these outcomes? No; and it will probably make things worse, for two reasons: (1) Longevity of team members; and (2) Inadequate time for training proficiency. Thus, TCP is a holistic and simple process that can rapidly on-board new team members and seamlessly integrate them into the organization's workflow.

Chapters 5 and 6 will discuss, respectively, the two foundational aspects of TCP: (1) the *Four Dynamics of Team Collaboration*; and (2) the *Six Steps of Team Collaboration*. Under these constructs, team leaders can identify and outline boundaries for each team member's role, and set the conditions for yielding the two distinct outcomes: High Satisfaction and High Performance. On the surface, TCP may look like just another "formula for success." However, with persistent and disciplined application, TCP will take a team's performance to new heights.

Chapter 5:
The Four Dynamics of
Team Collaboration

How can you ignite your team's potential in the face of modern challenges? In today's fast-paced, hyper-connected world, businesses face a number of challenges: disruptive technologies, fierce competition, and a workforce that yearns to find purpose. Teams are often bogged down by miscommunication, a lack of shared vision, and difficulty adapting to change.

This is where **AMMO** comes in. AMMO isn't just another acronym or corporate buzzword; it's a battle-tested framework to create high-performing teams that thrive in adversity.

A *wareness*
M *eaning*
M *aneuverability*
O *wnership*

1) **Awareness:** Sharpen your team's senses. Foster a deep understanding of individual strengths, weaknesses, and motivations. Build a culture of transparency where information flows freely, empowering everyone to make informed decisions.

2) **Meaning:** Unleash the power of purpose. Connect every team member to the bigger picture. When people understand how their work contributes to a shared mission, they become more engaged, innovative, and resilient.

3) **Maneuverability:** Equip your team to navigate the chaos. Cultivate agility and adaptability. Break down silos and foster collaboration so your team can pivot quickly in response to challenges.

4) **Ownership:** Empower your team to take charge. Encourage autonomy and accountability. When individuals feel ownership over their work, they become invested in the team's success and driven to exceed expectations.

AMMO isn't just about overcoming challenges; it's about unleashing your team's full potential. By fostering awareness, meaning, maneuverability, and ownership, you'll build a cohesive unit that's ready to tackle any obstacle and seize every opportunity.

We'll delve deeper into each element of AMMO, exploring practical strategies and real-world examples of how this framework can revolutionize your team's performance. Get ready to transform your team into a well-oiled machine, firing on all cylinders.

#1 Awareness

#1 Awareness: The Multifaceted Lens of Team Success

Awareness is the honed blade that pierces the veil of ambiguity, granting teams clarity and empowering them to make decisions with unwavering resolve. In the complex ecosystem of team dynamics, awareness is the multifaceted lens through which we perceive, interpret, and respond to the world around us. It illuminates our understanding of ourselves, our teammates, and the ever-shifting landscape in which we operate.

> *"The only true wisdom is in knowing you know nothing."*
> — *Socrates*

The Human Element of Awareness:
From Isolation to Interconnectedness

Imagine a team where individuals function as isolated atoms, their unique perspectives and talents shrouded in darkness. They stumble through projects, their efforts hampered by miscommunication, misunderstandings, and missed opportunities. They are a collection of disparate parts, failing to coalesce into a unified whole.

Now envision a team bathed in the radiant light of awareness. Each member is attuned to the nuances of their colleagues' communication styles, emotional states, and unspoken needs. They anticipate challenges, offer support proactively, and leverage collective wisdom to forge innovative solutions. Like a finely tuned instrument, their individual strengths harmonize, creating a symphony of productivity and success.

Consider the case of Sarah, a project manager leading a cross-functional team. Initially, her team struggled with misaligned priorities and conflicting goals. But by intentionally cultivating awareness, Sarah fostered an environment where open communication and mutual understanding thrived. Team members learned to appreciate each other's unique contributions, anticipate potential roadblocks, and proactively address conflicts.

The result?
A team that consistently delivered projects on time, under budget, and with exceptional quality.

#1 Awareness: The Perils of Ignorance: A Descent into Dysfunction

When awareness is neglected, teams descend into a perilous realm of ignorance. They operate on assumptions, react impulsively, and fail to recognize the subtle cues that signal impending disaster. The consequences can be severe, ranging from missed deadlines and budget overruns to a toxic work environment and a mass exodus of talent.

Picture a sales team struggling to meet their quarterly targets. Unaware of the evolving needs of their customers, they persist with outdated tactics and irrelevant messaging. Their sales figures plummet, morale craters, and the company's reputation suffers. This is the perilous terrain of ignorance, a self-inflicted wound that could have been avoided with a heightened sense of awareness.

Cultivating Awareness: A Multi-Sensory Approach

The good news is that awareness isn't an innate gift bestowed upon a select few; it's a skill that can be honed and refined through deliberate practice. By adopting a multi-sensory approach, we can elevate our awareness and unlock the full potential of our teams.

Types of Awareness:

1) **Self-Awareness:** The foundation of all awareness, it involves understanding our own strengths, weaknesses, biases, and triggers. By cultivating self-awareness, we become better equipped to manage our emotions, communicate effectively, and build stronger relationships.

> *"Awareness is the first step to victory."*
> — *Charles Spurgeon*

2) **Social Awareness:** This involves understanding the emotions, needs, and perspectives of others. It's about reading nonverbal cues, listening actively, and empathizing with our colleagues' experiences.

3) **Situational Awareness:** This encompasses a broader understanding of the context in which we operate – the

industry landscape, market trends, competitor activities, and internal dynamics within our organization. It enables us to anticipate challenges, seize opportunities, and make informed decisions.

Strategies for Cultivating Awareness:

- **Active Listening and Empathy:** Go beyond simply hearing the words spoken; listen for the underlying emotions and motivations. Seek to understand, not just to respond.
- **360-Degree Feedback:** Create a culture where feedback flows freely in all directions – from managers to employees, peer-to-peer, and even upward feedback. This fosters transparency, continuous improvement, and mutual respect.
- **Shared Experiences and Team-Building:** Invest in activities that promote bonding and shared experiences outside of the workplace. This builds camaraderie, trust, and a deeper understanding of each other's personalities and strengths.
- **Data-Driven Insights:** Utilize tools and technologies that provide real-time data, environmental scanning, and analytics on team performance, communication patterns, and project progress. Stay informed about industry trends, competitor activities, and emerging technologies. Understand the broader context in which your team operates and anticipate potential challenges or opportunities. These objective insights can reveal blind spots, uncover hidden strengths, and inform decision-making.
- **Mindfulness and Reflection:** Encourage your team to practice mindfulness, taking time to reflect on their thoughts, feelings, and biases. This self-awareness can lead to greater empathy, improved communication, and a more cohesive team dynamic.

The Fruits of Awareness:

When awareness is woven into the fabric of your team's culture, the benefits are profound and far-reaching. You'll witness a transformation from a collection of individuals to a symphony of collaboration, from reactive problem-solving to proactive innovation, from mediocrity to mastery.

Awareness is the fertile soil in which trust takes root, conflict finds resolution, and creativity flourishes. It empowers teams to navigate complexity with confidence, adapt to change with agility, and overcome challenges with resilience. It's not merely a soft skill; it's the cornerstone of high performance and the key to unlocking your team's full potential.

#2 Meaning

The "North Star" of a team's motivation is *Meaning*.

Meaning is the heart and soul of the AMMO framework – the driving force that fuels passion, engagement, and resilience within your team. It's the "why" behind the "what," the deeper purpose that connects individual tasks to a shared mission. When team members understand how their work contributes to a bigger picture, they become more than just employees; they become invested stakeholders in the success of the organization.

> *"The two most important days in your life are the day you are born and the day you find out why."*
> — *Mark Twain*

The Human Element of Meaning:
From Duty to Passion

Imagine a team that goes through the motions, simply completing tasks without understanding the broader impact of their work. They lack enthusiasm, struggle to find motivation, and often feel disconnected from the organization's goals. They're like sailors without a compass, drifting aimlessly at sea.

Now envision a team that's deeply connected to their

work's meaning. They understand how their individual contributions fit into the larger picture and see the tangible impact they're making. They're passionate, engaged, and driven to excel. They're like a crew with a clear destination, sailing confidently towards their shared goal.

Meet Emily, a customer service representative at a healthcare company. In the past, she felt her job was simply about answering phones and resolving complaints. But after her company launched a new initiative to connect employees with the patients they were helping, Emily's perspective changed. She heard stories of how her work directly improved people's lives, and her passion for her job soared. Emily became a vocal advocate for her team, eager to go above and beyond to ensure patients received the best possible care.

The Pitfalls of Meaninglessness

When work lacks meaning, the consequences are dire. Employees become disengaged, turnover rates rise, and productivity plummets. The cost of this disengagement isn't just financial; it's also human. When people feel their work lacks purpose, they lose motivation, experience burnout, and may even suffer from mental health issues.

Imagine a team of teachers who feel their work is undervalued and their impact is minimal. Their passion for education wanes, their energy dwindles, and they struggle to connect with their students. This creates a negative ripple effect, impacting not only the teachers themselves but also the students they're meant to inspire.

Create "Meaning" Reinforcements through Strategic Alignment

Cultivating meaning within your team isn't a matter of luck; it's a deliberate and strategic process. It involves aligning individual aspirations with organizational goals, communicating the impact of your team's work, and empowering individuals to connect with their own unique "why."

To achieve this alignment, leaders must first understand the interests of both decision-makers and consumers:

- **Decision-makers:** What are their goals, needs, and concerns? Are they focused on increasing profitability, expanding market share, or improving customer satisfaction? By understanding their motivations, you can frame your team's work in a way that resonates with their strategic objectives.

- **Consumers:** What are their needs, wants, and pain points? What problems are they trying to solve, and how can your team's work offer solutions? By understanding your customers' perspectives, you can connect your team's efforts to a greater purpose, one that benefits both the organization and the people it serves.

#2 Meaning: Leveraging Interests:

The final step in this multi-faceted approach to create meaning is to leverage the insights gleaned from decision-makers and consumers. Identify the common threads, the overlapping priorities, and the shared values that resonate with both groups.

For instance, if decision-makers seek cost reduction and consumers crave affordability, your team can focus on developing innovative solutions that deliver value at a competitive price point. If decision-makers desire increased efficiency and consumers yearn for a seamless user experience, your team can prioritize streamlining processes and simplifying interfaces.

#2 Meaning: The Symphony of Success

By interweaving the strategic goals of decision-makers with the desires of your consumers, you create a symphony of success. Your team's work becomes a harmonious blend of purpose, impact, and value. This not only fosters intrinsic motivation but also establishes your team as a vital asset to the organization.

When your team's efforts are aligned with both internal and external stakeholders, you unlock a powerful engine of growth. You maximize meaning, influence credibility, and drive tangible results that resonate with everyone involved. In this state of alignment, your team becomes more than just a group of individuals; they become a force for positive change, driving innovation, exceeding expectations, and leaving a lasting legacy.

Unleashing the Power of Meaning: A Leadership Opportunity

The good news is that cultivating meaning within your team isn't a mystery; it's a matter of conscious leadership. It's about creating a shared vision, communicating the impact of your team's work, and empowering individuals to connect with their own personal "why." How you can start infusing meaning into your team's work?

- **Craft a Compelling Vision:** Clearly articulate your organization's mission, values, and long-term goals. Paint a vivid picture of the future you're creating together and how each team member plays a vital role in that journey.
- **Connect the Dots:** Help your team members understand how their individual tasks contribute to the bigger picture. Show them the real-world impact of their work, whether it's improving customer satisfaction, developing innovative products, or making a positive difference in the community.
- **Encourage Personal Connection:** Empower your team members to explore their own personal 'why.' Encourage them to reflect on their passions, values, and how their work aligns with their individual goals.

- **Celebrate Milestones and Impact:** Regularly acknowledge and celebrate team achievements, both big and small. Highlight the positive impact your team is making and how their work is contributing to the organization's success.
- **Foster a Culture of Gratitude and Recognition:** Show appreciation for your team members' hard work and dedication. Recognize their individual contributions and create a culture where everyone feels valued and appreciated.

> *"Purpose is not something you find, it's something you build."*
>
> — *Tony Robbins*

More Than Motivation, It's a Strategic Imperative

When you tap into the power of meaning, the results are nothing short of transformative. Teams that understand the *why* behind their work don't just show up; they show out. They're not just engaged; they're electrified, fueled by a shared purpose that transcends individual tasks. Productivity soars as innovation flourishes, and challenges become opportunities for growth rather than obstacles to overcome.

This isn't just about warm, fuzzy feelings. Meaning is a strategic weapon, a competitive advantage that can't be easily replicated. Organizations that prioritize meaning attract top talent who crave more than just a paycheck. They retain these high performers because they've created a workplace where people feel valued, empowered, and connected to something bigger than themselves. And this translates directly to the bottom line, with increased productivity, higher customer satisfaction, and ultimately, greater profitability.

But the impact of meaning doesn't stop there. It extends beyond the walls of your organization, rippling out into the world. Teams driven by purpose are more likely to create products and services that resonate with customers on a deeper level. These teams are more likely to make ethical decisions that prioritize long-term sustainability over short-term gains and to contribute to their communities in meaningful ways.

When you invest in meaning, you're not just building a team; you're igniting a movement. You're fostering a culture where people are passionate about their work, committed to excellence, and driven to make a difference. This is the kind of environment that attracts top talent, drives innovation, and ultimately, changes the world.

So, as a leader, ask yourself: What is the deeper purpose behind your team's work? How can you connect individual tasks to a larger mission that resonates with your employees? By unlocking the power of meaning, you can unleash the full potential of your team and create a workplace that's both fulfilling and impactful. Remember, your team isn't just a collection of individuals; it's a force for change, ready to make its mark on the world.

> *"Morale is the single greatest factor in successful wars"*
> — *Dwight D. Eisenhower*

#3 Maneuverability

#3 Maneuverability: Navigating the Rapids of Change

In the tumultuous landscape of modern business, where disruption is the norm and change is constant, maneuverability is not just an advantage, it's a necessity. It's the ability of your team to adapt, pivot, and innovate in the face of unexpected

> *"It is not the strongest of the species that survives, nor the most intelligent that survives. It is the one that is most adaptable to change."*
> — *Charles Darwin*

challenges and new opportunities. It's about embracing agility, fostering collaboration, and empowering your team to navigate the rapids of change with confidence and grace.

The Human Element of Maneuverability: From Rigidity to Resiliency

Imagine a team that's rigid and inflexible, clinging to outdated processes and resisting new ideas. They're like a ship with a broken rudder, unable to navigate the stormy seas of change. They become frustrated, disengaged, and ultimately, left behind.

But consider a team that embraces maneuverability. They're like a nimble sailboat, adjusting their sails to catch the wind and changing course as needed. They thrive in the face of uncertainty, adapting to new challenges with ease and emerging stronger with each obstacle they overcome.

Meet James, a project manager at a marketing agency. When a major client unexpectedly changed their campaign direction, James's team initially panicked. But James had fostered a culture of agility, where open communication, cross-functional collaboration, and quick decision-making were valued. Together, they brainstormed new ideas, reallocated resources, and adjusted their timelines. In the end, they not only delivered a successful campaign but also strengthened their bond as a team.

The Pitfalls of Inflexibility

When teams lack maneuverability, they become victims of their own rigidity. They're slow to respond to market shifts, resistant to new technologies, and unable to capitalize on emerging opportunities. This inflexibility breeds frustration, stifles innovation, and ultimately, damages the bottom line.

Imagine a retail company that clings to its traditional brick-

and-mortar model, ignoring the growing trend of online shopping. As their competitors thrive in the digital marketplace, they struggle to keep up, losing customers and market share. This is the consequence of neglecting maneuverability – a slow and painful decline into irrelevance.

Cultivating Agile Leaders: A Team Transformation

The good news is that maneuverability isn't an innate trait; it's a skill that can be developed and honed. By implementing the right strategies and fostering a culture of agility, you can transform your team into a nimble, adaptable powerhouse. How can you start building a more maneuverable team?

- **Embrace Change as a Constant:** Instead of fearing change, view it as an opportunity for growth and innovation. Encourage your team to experiment, take risks, and learn from their mistakes.
- **Foster Cross-Functional Collaboration:** Break down silos and encourage communication and collaboration across different departments and teams. This allows for a broader perspective, faster decision-making, and more creative solutions.
- **Empower Decision-Making at All Levels:** Don't centralize all decision-making power at the top. Empower your team members to make decisions within their areas of expertise, trusting their judgment and providing support when needed.
- **Prioritize Learning and Development:** Invest in training and development programs that focus on agility, adaptability, and problem-solving skills. Encourage your team members to continuously learn and grow.
- **Celebrate Quick Wins and Adaptations:** Recognize and reward quick wins and successful adaptations. This reinforces the importance of agility and creates a positive feedback loop that encourages further innovation.

The Competitive Edge of Maneuver Leaders

In today's fast-paced business environment, maneuverability is no longer a luxury; it's a competitive necessity. Teams that can adapt to change, embrace new ideas, and pivot quickly are the ones that will thrive in the face of uncertainty.

By fostering a culture of agility, empowering your team to make decisions, and prioritizing learning and development, you can unlock your team's full potential and gain a significant competitive edge. Remember, in the world of business, it's not always the strongest or the smartest that survive; it's the most adaptable.

#4 Ownership

#4 Ownership: The Engine of Empowered Teams.

Imagine a workplace where every team member isn't just an employee, but a stakeholder. They don't merely execute tasks; they own them. They see challenges not as roadblocks, but as opportunities to innovate and excel. This is the power of ownership, the final pillar of the AMMO framework – a force that can transform your team from a collection of individuals into a high-performing, unstoppable unit.

The Human Element of Ownership: From Cogs to Captains

Ownership isn't just a concept; it's a feeling. It's the spark that ignites passion, the fuel that drives innovation, and the compass that guides decision-making. When people feel ownership, they stop being passive occupants and become active captains of their own ship.

Meet Sarah, a marketing coordinator at a tech startup. In the past, she felt like a cog in the machine, simply following orders and completing tasks. But when her manager entrusted her with leading a new campaign, everything changed. Sarah had the freedom to brainstorm ideas, make decisions, and own the results. Her creativity flourished, her confidence soared, and she became a vocal advocate for her project. This newfound ownership transformed Sarah from a dutiful employee into a passionate leader, eager to push boundaries and exceed expectations.

> *"The greatest leaders mobilize others by making them feel powerful."*
>
> *— Ben Zander*

The Pitfalls of Neglecting Ownership

But what happens when ownership is neglected? When teams lack autonomy, accountability, and the freedom to shape their work, a dark cloud descends. Engagement plummets, creativity stagnates, and a sense of helplessness takes hold.

Imagine a team of software engineers tasked with developing a new product. They're brilliant minds, bursting with ideas, but their manager micromanages every detail, stifling their creativity and crushing their motivation. Frustration mounts, innovation grinds to a halt, and top talent starts looking for the exit. This is the high cost of neglecting ownership – a downward spiral of disengagement, missed opportunities, and ultimately, lost profits.

#4 Ownership - Empowering Your Team: A Leadership Imperative

The good news is that fostering ownership isn't rocket science; it's a conscious choice. It's about shifting your mindset from control to empowerment, from micromanagement to trust. It's about seeing your team members not as subordinates, but as capable leaders in their own right. How you can start building a culture of ownership today?

- **Delegate with Purpose:** Don't just dump tasks on your team; delegate projects that align with their skills and interests. Give them the autonomy to explore solutions, make decisions, and own the outcome.
- **Set Clear Expectations and Provide Support:** While autonomy is crucial, ensure your team has a clear understanding of the goals, deadlines, and available resources. Offer guidance and feedback, but resist the urge to take over.
- **Celebrate Wins and Learn from Losses:** Recognize and reward individual and team achievements. When things don't go as planned, focus on learning and growth, not blame. Encourage experimentation and risk-taking, knowing that failures can be

valuable stepping stones to success.

- **Cultivate a Culture of Trust:** Trust is the cornerstone of ownership. Believe in your team's abilities, give them the space to make mistakes, and encourage them to take calculated risks. Celebrate their successes and support them through challenges.
- **Foster Feedback and Growth:** Encourage regular feedback sessions, both from you and among team members. This creates a culture of continuous improvement and reinforces ownership of individual and team development.

The Domino Effect of Empowerment

When you empower your team to take ownership, the benefits ripple through your organization. You'll see increased collaboration, enhanced problem-solving, improved morale, and ultimately, a team that's more engaged, productive, and innovative.

Remember, ownership isn't just about delegating tasks; it's about unlocking the full potential of your team. It's about creating a workplace where people feel valued, empowered, and excited to contribute their best. By embracing the power of ownership, you'll not only transform your team's performance but also build a more fulfilling and rewarding workplace for everyone.

Figure 5: Four Pillars of Team Synergy

Chapter 6:
The Six Steps of Team Collaboration

On the modern battlefield of high-stakes endeavors –
whether a military campaign, a complex business venture, or a
daring scientific exploration – victory doesn't often hinge on
the brilliance of one individual, but on the harmonious
interplay of a well-coordinated team. Like a symphony
orchestra, where each musician contributes their unique talent
to create a masterpiece, a successful team requires a
synchronized effort, a shared understanding of the objective,
and a well-defined process to navigate the complexities of the
journey.

This chapter unveils the Six Steps of Team Collaboration, a
battle-tested framework designed to empower teams to
achieve peak performance and unwavering satisfaction.
Drawing inspiration from the military's decision-making
process, coupled with project management decision-making,
and infused with the principles of collaborative leadership, this
framework provides a roadmap for navigating the often-
turbulent waters of teamwork.

From the initial "Orient" phase, where the team establishes
a shared vision and strategic direction, to the final
"Consolidate" phase, where lessons are learned (and a legacy
of continuous improvement is established), TCP guides teams
through a structured and collaborative process. It empowers
them to harness their collective intelligence, creativity, and
expertise to achieve extraordinary results.

Whether you are a seasoned leader or a new team member
embarking on your first collaborative journey, the Six Steps of
Team Collaboration offer a powerful toolkit for unlocking the
full potential of your team. By embracing this framework, you

can transform your team into a cohesive unit, capable of overcoming any challenge and achieving remarkable success.

Prepare to equip yourself for a rewarding journey, where collaboration becomes a powerful force for innovation, growth, and lasting achievement. The Six Steps of Team Collaboration await, ready to guide your team towards a future of shared success.

Step 1: Orient

Step 1: Orient - Understanding the Landscape

The first step of any collaborative endeavor is crucial. This is the time for the team to come together, not just as individual contributors, but as a cohesive unit with a shared understanding of the mission, the task organization (who's responsible for what), the overall timeline, and the expected end state.

Step 1 is often filled with a mix of excitement and anxiety. Team members may be eager to get started, but also apprehensive about the challenges that lie ahead. It's important to create a safe space where everyone feels comfortable asking questions, sharing concerns, and expressing their ideas.

Step 1: Orient - Common Pitfalls

- **Lack of Clarity:** If the mission or objectives are not clearly defined, it can lead to confusion, misalignment, and wasted effort.
- **Unrealistic Expectations:** Overly optimistic timelines or resource constraints can set the team up for failure.
- **Personality Clashes:** Early tensions or personality clashes can derail the team before it even gets started.

How to Accomplish Orientation:

1. **Kick-Off Meeting:** Hold a kick-off meeting to introduce the team members, review the mission statement, and establish a shared understanding of the goals.
2. **Open Dialogue:** Encourage open and honest communication. Allow team members to ask questions, share concerns, and challenge assumptions.
3. **Clear Roles and Responsibilities:** Clearly define roles and responsibilities for each team member, ensuring

everyone understands their part in the larger mission.

4. **Realistic Timeline:** Develop a realistic timeline with measurable milestones, taking into account potential risks and challenges.

5. **WARNORD 1:** Issue a formal warning order that summarizes the mission, task organization, timeline, and any initial guidance.

Step 1: Orient - Success Criteria

Before moving to the next step, the team should have:

- A clear and shared understanding of the mission and its purpose.
- Defined roles and responsibilities for each team member.
- A realistic timeline with measurable milestones.
- A formal WARNORD 1 issued to all stakeholders and/or members.
- A sense of shared purpose and excitement for the project.

Step 2: Analysis

Step 2: Analysis - Gathering Intelligence

In the analysis step, the team embarks on a journey of discovery. Think of it as a detective investigation, where the team gathers clues and pieces together the puzzle to gain a deeper understanding of the situation at hand. This involves conducting market research, analyzing the competition, identifying potential risks and opportunities, and breaking down the project into smaller, more manageable tasks.

Step 2 requires a blend of curiosity, skepticism, and collaboration. Team members need to be willing to challenge assumptions, dig deeper into the data, and work together to identify potential blind spots or biases.

Step 2: Analysis - Common Pitfalls

- **Information Overload:** Too much information can be just as detrimental as too little. Focus on gathering the most relevant and actionable data.
- **Analysis Paralysis:** Overthinking and overanalyzing can lead to delays and indecision. Set deadlines for analysis and make decisions based on the best available information.
- **Confirmation Bias:** The tendency to seek out information that confirms our existing beliefs can lead to flawed conclusions. Encourage the team to challenge their own assumptions and consider alternative viewpoints.

How to Accomplish Analysis:

1. **Information Gathering:** Conduct thorough research using a variety of sources, including market reports, customer surveys, competitor analysis, and expert interviews.
2. **Data Analysis:** Use data analysis tools and techniques to

identify trends, patterns, and correlations.

3. **Brainstorming:** Engage in brainstorming sessions to generate ideas, identify potential risks, and explore different scenarios.

4. **SWOT Analysis:** Conduct a SWOT (Strengths, Weaknesses, Opportunities, Threats) analysis to assess the team's internal and external environment.

5. **WARNORD 2:** Issue the second formal warning order to reflect the findings of the analysis step. This should be "good" enough to operate from within its clear task and purpose.

Step 2: Analysis - Success Criteria

Before moving to the next step, the team should have:

- A comprehensive understanding of the market, competition, and potential risks/opportunities.
- A detailed breakdown of tasks and responsibilities.
- A WARNORD 2 that reflects the team's current understanding of the adversarial situation, and each department's task, purpose, and end-state for the mission.
- A sense of confidence and clarity about the challenges and opportunities that lie ahead.

Step 3: Develop

Step 3: Develop - Crafting the Blueprint

With a solid understanding of the landscape, the team can now enter the develop step. This is where the raw data and insights gathered in the previous step are transformed into actionable plans. Think of it like an architect drafting blueprints for a building, carefully considering every detail, from the foundation to the finishing touches.

Step 3 is often characterized by a surge of creativity and collaboration. Team members bring their diverse perspectives and expertise to the table, brainstorming innovative solutions and exploring different approaches. It's a time of excitement and possibility, as the team envisions what could be.

Step 3: Develop - Common Pitfalls

- **Groupthink:** The desire for harmony can lead to premature consensus and the suppression of dissenting opinions. Encourage healthy debate and constructive criticism.
- **Lack of Focus:** Trying to tackle too many ideas at once can lead to confusion and lack of progress. Prioritize the most promising solutions and focus on refining them.
- **Ignoring Feasibility:** It's easy to get caught up in the excitement of brainstorming, but it's important to consider the practicalities of each idea. Evaluate the feasibility of each solution in terms of time, resources, and technical capabilities.

How to Accomplish Development:

1. **Brainstorming:** Engage in structured brainstorming sessions to generate a wide range of potential solutions.
2. **Idea Evaluation:** Evaluate each idea based on its potential impact, feasibility, and alignment with the team's goals.

3. **Prototype and Test:** Develop prototypes or mockups of the most promising solutions and test them with potential users or stakeholders.

4. **Iterate and Refine:** Based on feedback and testing, refine the solutions and iterate until they meet the team's requirements.

Step 3: Develop - Success Criteria

Before moving to the next step, the team should have:

- A well-developed tentative plan with multiple courses of action (COAs).
- A thorough understanding of the potential impacts and risks of each COA.
- A clear vision of the desired end state and the steps required to achieve it.
- A shared sense of ownership and excitement for heading into the evaluation with the developed courses of actions.

Step 4: Evaluate

Step 4: Evaluate - Making Informed Choices

The evaluate step is a critical juncture in the collaborative process. It's where the team transitions from ideation to decision-making. Think of it as a jury deliberating a verdict, carefully weighing the evidence, considering different perspectives, and ultimately reaching a consensus.

Step 4 can be fraught with tension and disagreement. It's natural for team members to have different opinions and preferences, but it's important to foster an environment of respectful debate and constructive criticism.

Step 4: Evaluate - Common Pitfalls

- **Decision Paralysis:** The fear of making the wrong choice can lead to inaction and missed opportunities. Set clear deadlines for decision-making and encourage the team to trust their judgment.
- **Hidden Agendas:** Personal biases or hidden agendas can cloud judgment and lead to suboptimal decisions. Encourage transparency and open communication to ensure everyone is working towards the same goals.
- **Lack of Stakeholder Input:** Failing to consider the perspectives of key stakeholders can lead to decisions that are not well-received or that fail to address critical needs. Engage stakeholders early and often in the decision-making process.

How to Accomplish Evaluation:

1. **Comparative Analysis:** Conduct a thorough analysis of each course of action (COA), comparing their strengths, weaknesses, opportunities, and threats.
2. **Risk Assessment:** Identify and assess the risks associated with each COA, developing mitigation strategies as needed.

3. **Cost-Benefit Analysis:** Weigh the costs and benefits of each COA, considering both short-term and long-term impacts.
4. **Decision Matrix:** Use a decision matrix to systematically evaluate each COA based on pre-determined criteria.
5. **Stakeholder Engagement:** Gather feedback from key stakeholders and incorporate their perspectives into the decision-making process.
6. **OPORD:** Issue the formal operations order, clearly conveying the selected course of action.

Step 4: Evaluate - Success Criteria

Before moving to the next step, the team should have:

- A clear and definitive decision on the chosen COA.
- A comprehensive OPORD that outlines the plan in detail, including roles, responsibilities, timelines, and contingency plans.
- Buy-in and commitment from all team members and stakeholders.
- A shared sense of confidence in the chosen path forward.
- OPORD that clearly conveys the decided strategy or COA and updated timeline.

Step 5: Maneuver

Step 5: Maneuver - Execution and Adaptation

The maneuver step is where the rubber meets the road – where theory becomes practice. This is the stage where the meticulously crafted plan is put into action. Imagine a well-trained military unit executing a complex operation, each member moving in sync, their actions guided by a shared understanding of the mission and their individual roles.

Step 5 is often characterized by a mix of adrenaline and focus. Team members are energized by the opportunity to put their skills and knowledge to the test, but they must also remain vigilant and adaptable to the inevitable challenges that arise.

Step 5: Maneuver - Common Pitfalls

- **Overconfidence:** A false sense of security can lead to complacency and a failure to anticipate potential problems. Encourage the team to remain vigilant and adaptable.
- **Lack of Communication:** As the plan unfolds, it's crucial to maintain open lines of communication. Miscommunication, or a breakdown in communication, can lead to confusion, delays, and missed opportunities.
- **Rigidity:** Sticking rigidly to the plan in the face of unexpected challenges can be disastrous. Encourage the team to be flexible and adaptable, willing to adjust their approach as needed.

How to Accomplish Maneuverability:

1. **Briefing and Rehearsal:** Ensure all team members understand the OPORD and their individual roles. Conduct rehearsals to practice the plan and identify potential issues.
2. **Clear Communication Channels:** Establish clear and effective communication channels to ensure everyone is

informed of progress, challenges, and changes.

3. **Monitoring and Evaluation:** Continuously monitor progress against the OPORD, track key metrics, and gather feedback from team members and stakeholders.

4. **Adaptability:** Be prepared to adjust the plan as needed in response to unforeseen challenges or opportunities.

5. **Celebrate Successes:** Take time to acknowledge and celebrate milestones and achievements along the way. This helps to maintain morale and motivation.

Step 5: Maneuver - Success Criteria

The maneuver step is successful when:

- The operational order's <u>intent</u> is executed effectively and efficiently.
- The team remains flexible and adaptable, able to respond to unforeseen challenges.
- The team achieves its objectives and meets or exceeds expectations.
- Morale remains high and team members feel a sense of accomplishment.

Step 6: Consolidate

Step 6: Consolidate - Learning and Improving

The consolidate step is the final stage of the collaborative process. Think of it as a post-game analysis, where the team gathers to reflect on their performance, identify lessons learned, and chart a course for future improvement.

Step 6 is a time for reflection, celebration, and growth. Team members should feel a sense of pride in their accomplishments, but also a willingness to acknowledge areas where they can improve.

Step 6: Consolidate - Common Pitfalls

- **Skipping the AAR:** Failing to conduct a thorough after-action review (AAR) can lead to missed opportunities for learning and growth; Also, you lose maximizing the joy of victories hard won!
- **Blame Game:** Focusing on blame rather than identifying lessons learned can create a toxic environment and hinder future collaboration.
- **Lack of Follow-Through:** Identifying areas for improvement is only the first step. Failing to implement changes can lead to repeating the same mistakes in the future.

How to Accomplish Consolidation:

1. **After-Action Review (AAR):** Conduct a comprehensive AAR to analyze what went well, what didn't, and why. Encourage open and honest feedback from all team members. This demands everyone's input; no one is a bystander.
2. **Lessons Learned:** Document key takeaways from the AAR and share them with the wider organization.
3. **SOP Updates:** Revise and update standard operating procedures (SOPs) to incorporate lessons learned.

4. **Action Plan:** Develop an action plan to address areas for improvement and implement changes.

5. **Celebrate Success:** Take time to celebrate the team's achievements and recognize individual contributions. Make it a formal event to reflect and celebrate shared achievements.

Step 6: Consolidate - Success Criteria

The consolidate step is successful when:

- The team has a clear understanding of its strengths and weaknesses.
- Lessons learned are documented and shared with the wider organization.
- SOPs are updated to reflect new knowledge and best practices.
- The team is committed to continuous improvement and ready to apply what they've learned to future projects.
- The team celebrates their success and recognizes the value of their collective efforts.

The Maneuver Model -
A Compass for Team Collaborative Process

The Maneuver Model, visually represented by the interconnected diamonds, encapsulates the essence of effective team collaboration. The central star, representing the Team Leaders, is surrounded by the six crucial steps - Orient, Analyze, Develop, Evaluate, Maneuver, and Consolidate. The cyclical arrangement visually reinforces the iterative nature of the process, emphasizing the need for continuous adaptation and improvement. It's a powerful reminder that collaboration is not a linear path, but a dynamic journey of exploration and discovery.

This model, built on the foundation of Six Steps of Team Collaboration; Four Dynamics of Team Collaboration (Awareness, Meaning, Maneuverability, and Ownership - AMMO); and a unifying Team Leadership Philosophy, provides a comprehensive roadmap for navigating the complexities of teamwork. It empowers teams to harness their collective intelligence, creativity, and expertise to achieve extraordinary results.

The Maneuver Planning Cycle (MPC), with its elegant simplicity and powerful message, encapsulates the essence of effective team collaboration. MPC illustrates a continuous process of planning, execution, and assessment that enables teams to remain agile and responsive in the face of uncertainty.

Whether you are a seasoned leader or a new team member, the Maneuver Model is a powerful tool for unlocking your team's potential. By embracing this framework, you can transform your team into a cohesive unit, capable of overcoming any challenge and achieving remarkable success.

Figure 6: Maneuver Planning Cycle (MPC)

SYNCHRONIZING PLANS
AND DECISIONS

1 LEADERSHIP PHILOSOPHY
6 STEPS & 4 DYNAMICS

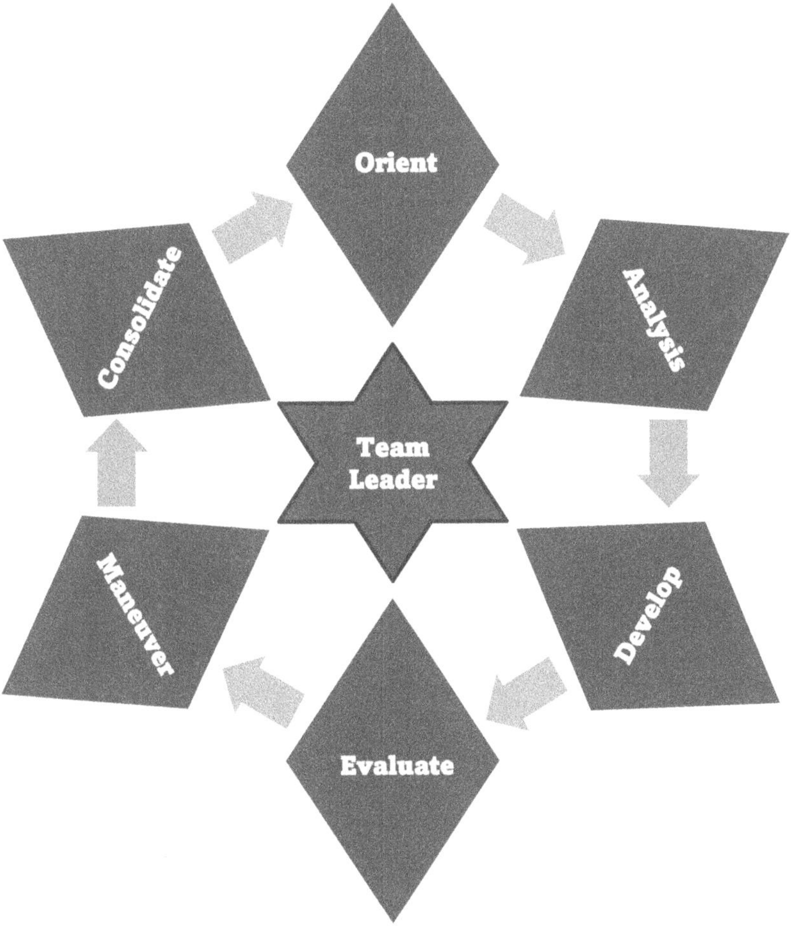

Chapter 7:
The Role of the Team Members

In the vast and ever-changing landscape of business, leadership is akin to captaining a ship through uncharted waters and treacherous fog. The success of any voyage hinges not only on the captain's skill but also on the unique talents and expertise of each crew member. Just as an exemplary crew is composed of diverse individuals, each with their own strengths and specializations, so too is a high-performing team.

This chapter invites you to reimagine your team as a cast of adventurer/explorer characters, each embodying a timeless archetype. We will delve into the seven essential character classes that every successful team needs to navigate the turbulent seas of the business world.

By understanding and embracing these archetypes, you can unlock the full potential of your team, foster a collaborative environment that thrives on diversity, and chart a course towards unparalleled success. Whether you're a seasoned leader or a new member setting sail, this chapter will equip you with the insights and tools you need to inspire a legendary crew, ready to conquer any challenge that comes their way.

Team Archetypes

"A ship is not a floating piece of wood, but a living being...with a soul and a will of its own." These words, attributed to Admiral Lord Nelson, echo the sentiment that a team (like a ship's crew) is more than the sum of its parts. It's a dynamic entity, driven by the collective will and expertise of its crew. In the turbulent seas of the business world, your team is your vessel, and each member plays a crucial role in navigating towards success.

Imagine your team not as mere employees, but as a legendary crew embarking on an odyssey. Each member embodies a timeless archetype, a character class whose strengths and skills are essential to charting the course, weathering storms, and ultimately reaching the shores of triumph. The seven archetypes discussed:

1. *Navigator:* - *Strategist*
2. *Quartermaster:* - *Planner*
3. *Alchemist:* - *Experimenter*
4. *Shipwright:* - *Engineer*
5. *Diplomat:* - *Communicator*
6. *Cartographer:* - *Analyst*
7. *Specialist:* - *Consultant*

1. The Navigator: Strategist

In the vast ocean of business, your team is a ship venturing into the unknown. At the helm stands the Navigator, the visionary leader whose unwavering determination and strategic vision steer the course. Like Odysseus, navigating the treacherous seas with cunning and resilience, or Captain Janeway from *Star Trek: Voyager*, boldly leading her crew through uncharted territory, the Navigator possesses the foresight to anticipate challenges, seize opportunities, and propel the team towards success.

The Navigator's role transcends mere decision-making; they are the architects of the team's shared purpose, the catalysts for innovation, and the anchors that steady the ship in the face of adversity. Their selfless leadership prioritizes the team's success above all else, fostering a collaborative environment where every member feels valued, heard, and empowered to contribute their unique talents. As such, navigators are often the decision-makers of the organization. And many other archetypes, once in the authoritative decision-making position, will resemble the Navigator's function. And natural talent, while attractive, is pale in contrast to a navigator who is skilled in asking the right questions.

At each stage of the Team Collaboration Process (TCP), the Navigator plays a distinct and indispensable role.

The Navigator: Strategist
Step 1: Orient - Setting the Course

The Navigator embarks on the collaborative journey by:

- **Crafting a Compelling Vision:** The Navigator doesn't just set a destination; they paint a vivid and inspiring picture of the future, one that resonates with the team's values and aspirations. This vision becomes the guiding star, illuminating the path forward and motivating the crew to achieve greatness. Like the ancient mariners who looked to the stars for guidance, the team looks to the Navigator's vision to steer their efforts. A strong vision statement is not merely a goal; it's an evocative picture of the future that excites and inspires the team. The Navigator's vision should be clear, concise, and emotionally resonant, capturing the hearts and minds of the team.

- **Mapping the Strategic Roadmap:** With a meticulous eye for detail and a deep understanding of the landscape, the Navigator charts a strategic roadmap. This roadmap outlines key milestones, potential obstacles, and alternative routes, serving as a flexible framework that can adapt to changing conditions. Like a seasoned cartographer, the Navigator anticipates challenges and ensures the team is prepared for the journey ahead. The roadmap should be clear and visual, providing a high-level overview of the project's trajectory and key decision points. It also needs to be flexible enough to allow for adjustments as the team gathers new information and encounters unforeseen obstacles.

- **Inspiring the Crew:** The Navigator doesn't simply dictate the course; they inspire the crew to embrace it. Through passionate communication, storytelling, and data-driven insights, they create a shared sense of purpose and excitement, ensuring that every team member understands their role and feels invested in the mission. The Navigator's communication should be clear, concise, and motivating, utilizing techniques such as storytelling, metaphors, and visual aids to convey the vision and inspire action. They create a culture of open communication where ideas are freely shared, and everyone feels heard.

The Navigator: Strategist
Step 2: Analyze - Navigating Seas of Information

The Navigator steers the team through analytical steps:

- **Leading Strategic Assessment:** Drawing on their deep understanding of the competitive landscape and market trends, the Navigator guides the team in analyzing the internal and external environment. They encourage critical thinking and open dialogue, ensuring all perspectives are considered in identifying strengths, weaknesses, opportunities, and threats (SWOT analysis). The Navigator challenges assumptions, probes for deeper understanding, and encourages the team to consider all angles before drawing conclusions.

- **Facilitating Scenario Planning:** The Navigator, with their ability to anticipate future scenarios, facilitates scenario planning exercises. They encourage the team to envision different outcomes and their potential impact on the project, fostering a proactive approach to risk management and preparedness. This process allows the team to develop contingency plans and prepare for the unexpected, ensuring they are ready to adjust course as needed.

- **Refining the Roadmap:** As the team gathers and analyzes information, the Navigator collaborates with them to refine the strategic roadmap. They ensure that the roadmap remains a living document, reflecting the team's evolving understanding of the landscape and adapting to new information or insights. The Navigator's flexibility and willingness to adjust the course based on data and analysis ensures the team remains agile and responsive to change, maximizing the chances of success.

The Navigator: Strategist
Step 3: Develop - Charting the Course to Innovation

The Navigator's visionary leadership shines through as they guide the team in developing innovative solutions:

- **Guiding Concept Ideation:** The Navigator encourages brainstorming and divergent thinking, fostering a creative environment where team members feel safe to share their ideas, no matter how unconventional. They champion a culture of innovation, encouraging the team to push boundaries and explore new possibilities. They facilitate brainstorming sessions that encourage a wide range of ideas and perspectives, ensuring that the team considers all possible solutions.

- **Ensuring Resource Alignment:** The Navigator works closely with the Quartermaster to ensure that the team's creative vision aligns with the available resources and constraints. They advocate for the necessary tools, funding, and support to bring the team's ideas to life. This collaboration ensures that the team's aspirations are grounded in reality and that their efforts are focused on achievable outcomes.

- **Defining Success Metrics:** The Navigator collaborates with the team to establish clear and measurable success criteria. This ensures that everyone understands what constitutes success and allows for objective evaluation of progress and outcomes. By setting clear goals and expectations, the Navigator helps the team stay focused and motivated. They ensure that these metrics are aligned with the overall vision and reflect the project's desired impact.

The Navigator: Strategist
Step 4: Evaluate - Making Informed Choices

The Navigator leads the team through the decision-making process with a strategic mindset:

- **Conducting Strategic Evaluation:** The Navigator leads the team in evaluating potential solutions and strategies through the lens of the overarching vision and long-term goals. They ensure that every decision aligns with the team's mission and values. This involves analyzing the potential risks and rewards of each option, considering the impact on stakeholders, and assessing the long-term consequences of each choice.

- **Facilitating Collaborative Decision-Making:** The Navigator creates an inclusive decision-making process, ensuring that all voices are heard and that the final decision is informed by a diversity of perspectives. They encourage open dialogue and debate, helping the team reach consensus on the best course of action. By fostering a collaborative decision-making process, the Navigator ensures that the team feels ownership of the chosen path and is committed to its success.

- **Mitigating Risks:** Working in tandem with the Quartermaster, the Navigator assesses potential risks associated with the chosen course of action. They develop contingency plans and mitigation strategies, ensuring the team is prepared for any challenges that may arise during implementation. This proactive approach to risk management helps to minimize disruptions and keep the project on track.

The Navigator's leadership is crucial during the implementation step:

- **Inspiring and Guiding:** The Navigator continues to motivate the team, reminding them of the vision and the impact of their work. They provide guidance and support, celebrating small victories and offering encouragement when facing setbacks. Their presence instills confidence and reinforces the team's commitment to the mission. By maintaining a positive and supportive environment, the Navigator ensures that the team remains engaged and focused on achieving their goals.

- **Adapting Strategically:** As the project unfolds, the Navigator remains vigilant, monitoring progress and adjusting the strategic roadmap as needed. They embrace change as an opportunity for growth and innovation, empowering the team to adapt to new information and unforeseen challenges. This flexibility allows the team to pivot quickly and respond effectively to changing circumstances, ensuring that they stay on course towards their objectives.

- **Course Correcting:** If the project veers off course, the Navigator steps in to provide guidance and realign the team with the vision. They are not afraid to make tough decisions, course-correcting as needed to ensure the team reaches its destination. The Navigator's ability to make decisive adjustments and steer the team back on track is crucial for overcoming obstacles and achieving success.

The Navigator: Strategist
Step 6: Consolidate - Reflecting on the Journey and Charting the Future

The Navigator leads the team in reflecting on the journey and preparing for the next adventure:

- **Leading Strategic Review:** The Navigator facilitates a comprehensive review of the project, analyzing its impact, identifying key learnings, and evaluating the effectiveness of the strategic roadmap. This reflective process allows the team to celebrate successes, learn from failures, and extract valuable insights for future endeavors. The Navigator encourages open and honest feedback, creating a safe space for team members to share their perspectives and contribute to the learning process.

- **Sharing Knowledge:** The Navigator ensures that lessons learned are documented and disseminated throughout the organization, fostering a culture of continuous learning and improvement. They encourage the team to share their experiences and insights, ensuring that valuable knowledge is captured and preserved for future projects. By creating a knowledge-sharing culture, the Navigator helps the organization build on its successes and avoid repeating past mistakes.

- **Envisioning the Future:** The Navigator looks beyond the current project, identifying new opportunities and setting ambitious goals for the future. They inspire the team to continue their journey of exploration and innovation, fostering a sense of excitement and anticipation for the next collaborative adventure. By constantly looking towards the future, the Navigator ensures that the team remains motivated, engaged, and ready to tackle new challenges.

The Navigator, with their strategic vision, inspirational leadership, and unwavering commitment to the team's success, is the guiding star that empowers the crew to navigate the complexities of the business.

2. The Quartermaster: Planner

"The difference between ordinary and extraordinary is that little extra." – Jimmy Johnson

The Quartermaster, akin to a seasoned ship's officer, is the unsung hero who keeps the collaborative voyage on course. They are the masters of logistics, the architects of order, and the guardians of resources. Like Mr. Sulu, meticulously managing the *Enterprise*'s complex systems, or Zoe Washburne, ensuring *Serenity*'s crew is equipped and ready for action, the Quartermaster's behind-the-scenes work is crucial for the team's success.

Beyond simply managing supplies, the Quartermaster is a proactive force, anticipating needs and analyzing potential obstacles before they arise. They maintain detailed records, track progress, and provide timely updates, ensuring everyone is aligned and informed. They visualize and understand how each component of the project is resourced, preventing potential bottlenecks and maximizing the team's potential.

Ultimately, the Quartermaster is an enabler. They empower the team by removing logistical burdens and providing the necessary tools and resources to achieve their goals. Their dedication to organization and efficiency allows others to focus on their core responsibilities, unleashing their creativity and productivity. They are the silent force that transforms potential into reality, making the extraordinary possible. Their ability to predict, organize, and facilitate ensures that every 'little extra' is accounted for, allowing the team to navigate complex projects with confidence and achieve exceptional outcomes.

The Quartermaster: Planner
Step 1: Orient - Setting Sail with a Detailed Map

The Quartermaster's journey begins with meticulous preparation, ensuring the team is well-equipped for the voyage ahead. This involves:

- **Charting the Timeline:** Like a skilled navigator plotting a course through treacherous waters, the Quartermaster crafts a comprehensive project timeline. This isn't just a list of dates; it's a dynamic roadmap that outlines key milestones, critical deadlines, and interdependencies between tasks. This meticulously crafted timeline serves as a visual representation of the project's trajectory, ensuring everyone understands the expectations and the journey ahead.

- **Inventorying and Allocating Resources:** With a keen eye for detail, the Quartermaster takes stock of the team's resources, including budget, personnel, and equipment. They carefully analyze the project's requirements and allocate resources accordingly, ensuring that the right tools are in the right hands at the right time. This strategic allocation minimizes waste and maximizes efficiency, setting the stage for a smooth and successful journey.

- **Preparing for the Unexpected:** The Quartermaster understands that the best-laid plans can encounter rough seas. They anticipate potential risks and challenges, identifying potential bottlenecks, resource shortages, or technical difficulties. Like a seasoned sailor battening down the hatches before a storm, the Quartermaster develops contingency plans and mitigation strategies, ensuring that the team is prepared for any unforeseen obstacles.

The Quartermaster: Planner
Step 2: Analyze - Navigating the Depths of Information

Armed with a wealth of data and insights, the Quartermaster refines the initial plan:

- **Diving Deep into Resource Analysis:** The Quartermaster leaves no stone unturned in assessing the availability and feasibility of required resources. They meticulously research vendors, negotiate contracts, explore alternative solutions, and reallocate existing resources as needed. This comprehensive analysis ensures that the team has the necessary tools and support to navigate the challenges ahead.
- **Refining the Financial Course:** Based on the analysis, the Quartermaster fine-tunes the budget, ensuring it aligns with the project's evolving needs and potential risks. This may involve making difficult trade-offs, reallocating funds, or finding creative solutions to maximize value and minimize costs.
- **Adjusting the Timeline with Precision:** If the analysis reveals unexpected challenges or delays, the Quartermaster swiftly revises the timeline. They communicate these changes transparently, ensuring that everyone understands the new expectations and can adapt their efforts accordingly.

The Quartermaster: Planner
Step 3: Develop - Constructing the Blueprint for Success

The Quartermaster transforms strategic vision into a concrete action plan:

- **Building a Detailed Implementation Plan:** The Quartermaster assembles the various pieces of the puzzle, creating a detailed plan that outlines specific tasks, responsibilities, timelines, and resource requirements for each step of the project. This meticulous blueprint serves as a guide for the team, ensuring that everyone knows their role and can execute their tasks effectively.

- **Crafting a Procurement Strategy:** If the project requires external resources or services, the Quartermaster takes charge of procurement, ensuring that the necessary items are acquired in a timely and cost-effective manner. They negotiate with vendors, manage contracts, and oversee the delivery of goods and services, ensuring that the team has everything it needs to succeed.

- **Anticipating the Unforeseen:** The Quartermaster remains vigilant, continuously evaluating the project's risk profile and updating contingency plans as needed. They stay ahead of potential challenges, ensuring that the team is prepared to adapt and pivot if necessary.

The Quartermaster: Planner
Step 4: Evaluate - The Critical Review

Before the team sets sail, the Quartermaster conducts a final review to ensure the ship is ready for the journey:

- **Assessing Feasibility and Viability:** The Quartermaster meticulously evaluates the implementation plan, considering all available resources, timelines, and potential risks. They identify any gaps or inconsistencies, proposing solutions to ensure the plan is realistic, achievable, and aligned with the team's goals.

- **Analyzing the Financial Investment:** They conduct a thorough cost-benefit analysis, weighing the financial investment against the expected return on investment. This ensures that the project is not only successful but also financially sound and sustainable.

- **Optimizing for Efficiency:** The Quartermaster continually seeks ways to optimize resource allocation, ensuring that every dollar and every hour is used effectively. This may involve renegotiating contracts, reallocating resources, or finding innovative ways to reduce costs without sacrificing quality.

The Quartermaster: Planner
Step 5: Maneuver - Steering Through Rough Waters

During the implementation step, the Quartermaster is the vigilant helmsman, keeping the ship on course and ensuring smooth sailing:

- **Tracking Resource Utilization:** The Quartermaster meticulously monitors the use of resources, ensuring they are being used efficiently and effectively. They identify any overages or shortages and make adjustments as needed, keeping the project within budget and on schedule.

- **Monitoring Progress and Milestones:** They track the project's progress against the timeline, celebrating milestones and identifying any bottlenecks or delays. They proactively address any issues that arise, ensuring that the project stays on track and meets its deadlines.

- **Implementing Risk Mitigation Strategies:** If unforeseen challenges arise, the Quartermaster activates the contingency plans they developed earlier. They remain calm under pressure, making sound decisions and guiding the team through any turbulent waters.

The Quartermaster: Planner
Step 6: Consolidate - Learning from the Journey

The voyage may be complete, but the Quartermaster's work continues. They ensure that the team learns and grows from the experience by:

- **Analyzing Resource Utilization:** The Quartermaster carefully reviews how resources were used throughout the project, identifying areas where efficiency can be improved in future endeavors. They share these insights with the team, fostering a culture of continuous improvement.
- **Documenting Lessons Learned:** They meticulously document the lessons learned regarding resource management, risk mitigation, and overall project execution. This valuable knowledge becomes a part of the team's institutional memory, ensuring that future projects benefit from the experiences of the past.
- **Recommending Process Improvements:** Based on the lessons learned, the Quartermaster proposes changes to processes and procedures, streamlining operations and enhancing the team's overall efficiency and effectiveness.

The Quartermaster, with their unwavering commitment to detail, efficiency, and resourcefulness, is the bedrock of any successful team. Their contributions ensure that the ship sails smoothly, the crew is well-prepared, and the journey towards success is both rewarding and sustainable.

3. The Alchemist: Experimenter

"The true sign of intelligence is not knowledge but imagination."
– Albert Einstein

In the heart of every high-performing team resides the Alchemist, the spark that ignites innovation and propels the group beyond the boundaries of the ordinary. Like Leonardo da Vinci, whose boundless curiosity and inventiveness transcended disciplines, or Kaylee Frye, the intuitive engineer who breathed life into *Serenity*'s engines, the Alchemist thrives in the realm of possibility. They are the dreamers and the doers, the ones who see potential where others see problems, and who dare to challenge the status quo.

The Alchemist's role extends far beyond simply generating ideas. They are the architects of transformation, the catalysts of change, and the champions of a creative culture. Their unique blend of curiosity, ingenuity, and adaptability empowers the team to navigate uncharted territories, overcome obstacles, and achieve breakthrough results.

At each stage of the Team Collaboration Process (TCP), the Alchemist plays a vital role in fostering a culture of creativity and innovation:

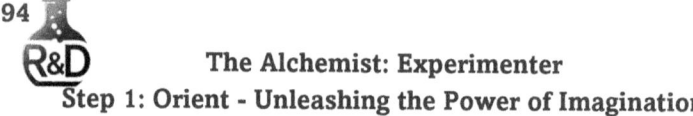

The Alchemist: Experimenter
Step 1: Orient - Unleashing the Power of Imagination

The Alchemist sets the stage for creative exploration by:

- **Envisioning Beyond the Horizon:** The Alchemist challenges the team to think beyond the confines of convention, to dream big, and to envision a future where anything is possible. Like a master illusionist, the Alchemist conjures a world of infinite possibilities, inspiring the team to break free from limiting beliefs and explore uncharted territories. The Alchemist's infectious enthusiasm and boundless optimism create a fertile ground for creativity to flourish.

- **Igniting the Spark of Ideation:** The Alchemist leads brainstorming sessions that are more akin to creative workshops than formal meetings. They encourage a free flow of ideas, where no thought is too outlandish and every contribution is valued. They create a safe space where team members feel empowered to share their wildest dreams, knowing that they will be met with curiosity and enthusiasm, not judgment. By cultivating a culture of openness and experimentation, the Alchemist ensures that no potential solution is overlooked.

- **Questioning Assumptions:** The Alchemist is the team's resident skeptic, always asking "why?" and "what if?". They challenge assumptions, provoke thought, and encourage the team to question the status quo. Their relentless curiosity and inquisitive nature spark new ideas and uncover hidden opportunities. By constantly pushing the boundaries of conventional thinking, the Alchemist helps the team discover innovative solutions that may have otherwise remained hidden.

The Alchemist: Experimenter
Step 2: Analyze - Transforming Data into Inspiration

The Alchemist sees data not just as numbers but as a source of inspiration:

- **Discerning Trends and Patterns:** The Alchemist is always on the lookout for emerging trends, technologies, and market shifts that could impact the project. They analyze this information through a creative lens, seeking inspiration for innovative solutions and strategies. Like a seasoned detective, they piece together clues from diverse sources, identifying patterns and connections that others may overlook. The Alchemist's ability to interpret data creatively allows them to uncover hidden opportunities and anticipate potential challenges.
- **Solving Problems Creatively:** The Alchemist approaches challenges as exciting puzzles to be solved. They apply their unique problem-solving skills to identify root causes, brainstorm creative solutions, and develop innovative strategies. They see obstacles as opportunities for growth and innovation, and they inspire the team to embrace the challenge of finding new and better ways to achieve their goals. By fostering a "can-do" attitude, the Alchemist helps the team overcome obstacles and transform setbacks into stepping stones.
- **Synthesizing Disparate Ideas:** The Alchemist has a knack for connecting seemingly unrelated concepts, finding patterns and correlations that others may miss. They weave together information from diverse sources, creating a tapestry of insights that leads to breakthrough ideas. Their ability to see the bigger picture and connect the dots is essential for generating truly innovative solutions that address the root cause of problems, rather than just the symptoms.

The Alchemist: Experimenter
Step 3: Develop - Bringing Ideas to Life

The Alchemist transforms ideas into tangible solutions by:

- **Crafting Innovative Concepts:** The Alchemist takes the raw insights and ideas generated during the analysis step and transforms them into tangible concepts and solutions. They are the architects of innovation, designing prototypes, mockups, and proof-of-concept models that bring ideas to life. The Alchemist's ability to visualize and articulate complex ideas in a way that is both inspiring and practical is essential for gaining buy-in and support from stakeholders. By bridging the gap between imagination and reality, the Alchemist ensures that the team's innovative ideas are not just theoretical but have the potential to be implemented and make a real impact.

- **Embracing Experimentation:** The Alchemist understands that the path to innovation is paved with trial and error. They encourage a culture of experimentation, where failure is seen as a learning opportunity and risk-taking is celebrated. They empower the team to try new things, to explore uncharted territories, and to learn from their mistakes. This fearless approach to experimentation fosters a spirit of innovation and continuous improvement, allowing the team to evolve and adapt in a rapidly changing environment.

- **Applying Design Thinking:** The Alchemist uses design thinking principles to empathize with users, define problems, ideate solutions, and iterate based on feedback. They ensure that the team's solutions are not only creative but also user-centered and practical. By incorporating user feedback and testing their ideas in real-world scenarios, the Alchemist ensures that the final product or service is not only innovative but also meets the needs and expectations of its intended audience.

The Alchemist: Experimenter
Step 4: Evaluate - Refining the Gold

R&D

The Alchemist doesn't just create; they refine. They evaluate the potential of creative solutions by:

- **Applying a Critical Eye:** The Alchemist objectively assesses each potential solution, considering its originality, novelty, and potential impact. They challenge the team to think beyond the obvious, pushing the boundaries of what's possible while maintaining a pragmatic focus on feasibility. They encourage the team to think critically about each idea, weighing its strengths and weaknesses against the project's goals and constraints.

- **Balancing Creativity and Feasibility:** The Alchemist collaborates with the Shipwright and other team members to ensure that creative solutions are not only innovative but also practical and achievable. They help the team balance their aspirations with the realities of resources, time, and technical limitations. By striking this balance, the Alchemist ensures that the team's creativity is channeled into solutions that can be realistically implemented and have a meaningful impact.

- **Iterating and Refining:** The Alchemist embraces feedback as a crucial part of the creative process. They encourage the team to iterate and refine their solutions based on input from stakeholders, user testing, and real-world results. This iterative approach allows the team to continuously improve their ideas, ensuring that the final product or service is the best it can be.

The Alchemist's flexibility shines as they guide the team through implementation:

- **Adapting to Change:** The Alchemist recognizes that the business landscape is constantly evolving and that creative solutions must be adaptable. They remain flexible and open-minded throughout the implementation step, adjusting the team's approach as needed to respond to unexpected challenges or opportunities. Their ability to think on their feet and pivot quickly ensures that the team can navigate the unpredictable terrain of the market.

- **Promoting Innovation:** The Alchemist is a tireless advocate for innovation, encouraging the team to embrace change and experiment with new approaches. They create a culture where risk-taking is celebrated and where new ideas are welcomed with open arms. By fostering a spirit of innovation, the Alchemist helps the team stay ahead of the curve and maintain a competitive edge.

- **Solving Problems Creatively:** When obstacles arise, the Alchemist sees them as opportunities to flex their creative muscles. They apply their problem-solving skills to find innovative solutions, often thinking outside the box and coming up with ideas that others might overlook. Their ability to remain calm under pressure and find creative solutions to problems is essential for keeping the project on track and achieving success.

The Alchemist: Experimenter
Step 6: Consolidate - Harvesting the Fruits of Innovation

R&D

The Alchemist ensures that the team's creative spirit continues to thrive by:

- **Creative Retrospection:** The Alchemist leads the team in reflecting on the creative process, identifying what worked well and what could be improved. They celebrate successes, analyze setbacks, and extract valuable lessons to inform future endeavors. This reflective practice not only fosters a culture of continuous improvement but also helps the team to build on their strengths and learn from their mistakes.
- **Knowledge Sharing:** The Alchemist is passionate about sharing their knowledge and expertise with others. They actively document and disseminate creative insights and lessons learned, ensuring that the team's collective wisdom is preserved and leveraged for future projects. By creating a knowledge-sharing culture, the Alchemist helps to build a sustainable pipeline of innovation within the organization.
- **Cultivating Continuous Innovation:** The Alchemist understands that innovation is not a one-time event but an ongoing process. They encourage the team to remain curious, adaptable, and open to new approaches, fostering a culture where creativity is valued and nurtured. By inspiring a love of learning and a thirst for knowledge, the Alchemist ensures that the team's creative spirit continues to thrive long after the project's completion.

The Alchemist, with their boundless creativity, unwavering optimism, and passion for innovation, is an invaluable asset to any team. Their presence not only sparks new ideas but also fosters a culture of continuous improvement and exploration. By embracing the Alchemist's spirit, teams can unlock their full potential, transform challenges into opportunities, and achieve unprecedented levels of success. The Alchemist's legacy is one of transformation, inspiring others to see.

4. The Shipwright: Engineer

"Quality is never an accident; it is always the result of intelligent effort." – John Ruskin

In the grand symphony of team collaboration, the Shipwright is the master craftsman, the one who transforms visions into tangible reality. Like Hephaestus, the Greek god of blacksmiths and craftsmen, they possess a meticulous attention to detail and a dedication to quality that is unmatched. Or, like Montgomery Scott, the resourceful engineer from *Star Trek*, they can improvise their way out of any technical challenge, ensuring that the ship—your project or initiative—remains seaworthy.

The Shipwright's role extends far beyond mere technical expertise. They are the guardians of quality, the pragmatic problem solvers, and the builders of reliable systems. Their contributions ensure that the team's work is not only innovative but also practical, efficient, and built to last.

At each stage of the Team Collaboration Process (TCP), the Shipwright plays a vital role in ensuring the team's efforts are well-grounded and structurally sound:

The Shipwright: Engineer
Step 1: Orient – Laying the Keel

The Shipwright begins the collaborative journey by meticulously laying the keel, the foundation upon which the team's success will be built:

- **Technical Feasibility Assessment:** Like a skilled architect surveying the land before construction, the Shipwright meticulously examines the project's requirements, identifying potential technical challenges, limitations, and opportunities. They assess the complexity of the task, the available technologies, and the resources required to bring the vision to life. This early assessment ensures that the team's aspirations align with reality and that the project is technically feasible within the given constraints.

- **Resource Inventory and Optimization:** The Shipwright takes stock of the team's toolbox, carefully assessing the available resources, technologies, and skills. They identify any gaps that need to be filled, ensuring that the team has the right tools for the job. Like a master carpenter selecting the finest wood for a ship's hull, the Shipwright seeks to optimize resource utilization, ensuring that the team operates efficiently and cost-effectively.

- **Skills Gap Analysis and Planning:** The Shipwright identifies any areas where the team's technical skills or knowledge may fall short. Like a seasoned mentor, they develop a plan to bridge these gaps, whether through training, mentorship, or the acquisition of additional expertise. This proactive approach ensures that the team is well-equipped to handle the technical challenges ahead.

The Shipwright: Engineer
Step 2: Analyze – Surveying the Seascape

The Shipwright strengthens the technical foundation by:

- **In-Depth Technical Research:** The Shipwright embarks on a voyage of discovery, diving deep into the technical aspects of the project. They research relevant technologies, tools, and methodologies, exploring the cutting edge of their field to ensure the team's approach is based on the latest knowledge and best practices. Like a seasoned sailor studying nautical charts, the Shipwright seeks to understand the currents and tides of the technological landscape, ensuring the team is well-prepared to navigate them.

- **Feasibility Analysis and Optimization:** With a pragmatic mindset, the Shipwright scrutinizes the feasibility of different technical approaches, considering factors like cost, time, resource constraints, and scalability. They seek to optimize the chosen approach, ensuring that it is not only effective but also efficient and sustainable. Like a shipbuilder refining a hull design for maximum speed and stability, the Shipwright seeks to balance innovation with practicality.

- **Technical Risk Assessment and Mitigation:** The Shipwright identifies and assesses potential technical risks that could threaten the project's success, such as software glitches, hardware failures, or security breaches. Like a vigilant lookout scanning the horizon for storms, the Shipwright anticipates these risks and develops mitigation strategies to minimize their impact. This proactive approach ensures that the team is prepared to weather any technical challenges that may arise.

The Shipwright: Engineer
Step 3: Develop – Blueprinting the Vision

The Shipwright translates concepts into tangible solutions by:

- **Crafting Technical Blueprints:** The Shipwright brings the team's vision to life by creating detailed technical specifications, blueprints, and design documents. These blueprints serve as a roadmap for implementation, guiding the team in building a solution that is not only functional but also elegant and efficient. Like a master architect designing a grand cathedral, the Shipwright meticulously plans every detail, ensuring that the final product is structurally sound and aesthetically pleasing.

- **Constructing Prototypes and Proof-of-Concepts:** The Shipwright builds prototypes or proof-of-concept models to test and validate the technical feasibility of the chosen solution. This iterative process allows for early identification of issues and ensures that the final product meets the desired specifications. Like a skilled engineer testing a new engine design, the Shipwright experiments and refines their creation, ensuring that it is both innovative and reliable.

- **Establishing Quality Assurance:** The Shipwright establishes rigorous quality assurance standards and procedures, ensuring that the final product or service meets the highest levels of excellence. They develop test plans, conduct thorough testing, and implement quality control measures to ensure that the team's creation is not only functional but also reliable, durable, and user-friendly. Like a master inspector ensuring the safety of a ship before it sets sail, the Shipwright ensures that the team's work is of the highest caliber.

The Shipwright: Engineer
Step 4: Evaluate – Ensuring Technical Soundness and Feasibility

The Shipwright ensures that the chosen solution is not only creative but also practical and feasible by:

- **Technical Evaluation:** The Shipwright rigorously evaluates the proposed solution against the established technical specifications and requirements, ensuring that it meets or exceeds expectations. This evaluation involves a comprehensive review of the design, functionality, and performance of the solution, identifying any potential flaws or weaknesses that need to be addressed.
- **Risk Mitigation:** The Shipwright works closely with the team to address any technical risks identified during the evaluation process. They develop and implement mitigation strategies, such as redundancy measures, fail-safes, and backup plans, to minimize the impact of these risks on the project's timeline and budget.
- **Technical Review with Stakeholders:** The Shipwright communicates the technical aspects of the solution to stakeholders in clear and concise terms, addressing any concerns or questions they may have. This ensures that stakeholders understand the technical implications of the chosen approach and have confidence in the team's ability to deliver a high-quality solution.

T&E

The Shipwright: Engineer
Step 5: Maneuver – Steering Implementation with Precision

The Shipwright ensures smooth implementation and troubleshooting by:

- **Technical Implementation:** The Shipwright leads the technical implementation of the chosen solution, overseeing the work of other technical team members and providing guidance and support as needed. They ensure that the implementation adheres to the established specifications and timelines, while also maintaining a focus on quality and efficiency.

- **Troubleshooting and Problem-Solving:** When technical challenges arise, the Shipwright steps in to diagnose and resolve issues quickly and effectively. They leverage their expertise and problem-solving skills to find creative solutions, minimizing downtime and ensuring the project stays on track. Their ability to troubleshoot under pressure is essential for keeping the ship sailing smoothly.

- **Quality Assurance Monitoring:** The Shipwright continuously monitors the quality of the implemented solution, conducting regular tests and inspections to ensure it meets the established standards. They identify any potential issues and take corrective action as needed, ensuring that the final product or service is reliable, durable, and user-friendly.

The Shipwright: Engineer
Step 6: Consolidate – Learning from the Voyage

The Shipwright ensures continuous improvement by:

- **Technical Post-Mortem:** The Shipwright conducts a thorough post-project technical review, analyzing the performance of the solution, identifying lessons learned, and documenting best practices. This valuable feedback informs future projects and helps the team continuously improve its technical capabilities.
- **Knowledge Sharing:** They actively share their technical knowledge and expertise with the team, mentoring and coaching other members to enhance their technical skills. This fosters a culture of learning and growth, ensuring that the team's technical capabilities remain sharp and up-to-date.
- **Process Optimization:** Based on the lessons learned, the Shipwright identifies opportunities to streamline processes, improve tools and technologies, and enhance the overall efficiency and effectiveness of the team's technical work. This continuous improvement mindset ensures that the team is always striving for excellence and is well-prepared to tackle future challenges.

The Shipwright, with their unwavering commitment to detail, efficiency, and resourcefulness, is the bedrock of any successful team. Their contributions ensure that the ship sails smoothly, the crew is well-prepared, and the journey towards success is both rewarding and sustainable.

5. The Diplomat: Communicator

"The most important thing in communication is to hear what isn't being said." – Peter Drucker

In the heart of every high-performing team resides the Diplomat, the master communicator and empathetic listener who fosters unity and harmony. Like Eleanor Roosevelt, whose grace and diplomacy earned her the title "First Lady of the World," the Diplomat possesses a unique gift for understanding and connecting with others.

The Diplomat's role transcends mere communication skills. They are the bridge builders, the conflict resolvers, and the champions of a positive team culture. Their ability to listen deeply, speak clearly, and foster understanding is the cornerstone of effective collaboration. The Diplomat creates a safe haven for open dialogue, ensuring that every voice is heard and every perspective is valued.

At each stage of the Team Collaboration Process (TCP), the Diplomat plays a crucial role in nurturing relationships, facilitating communication, and resolving conflicts:

The Diplomat: Communicator
Step 1: Orient – Establishing a Culture of Collaboration

The Diplomat sets the tone for a collaborative and inclusive environment by:

- **Fostering Connection and Trust:** Like a skilled host welcoming guests to a banquet, the Diplomat creates a warm and inviting atmosphere for the team. They initiate icebreakers, team-building activities, and social events to help team members connect on a personal level and build trust. They encourage open communication, create a safe space for sharing ideas and concerns, and promote a culture of mutual respect and appreciation.

- **Assessing Communication Styles:** Recognizing that effective communication is the cornerstone of collaboration, the Diplomat assesses the communication styles and preferences of each team member. They identify potential barriers to effective communication, such as language barriers, cultural differences, or personality clashes, and develop strategies to bridge those gaps.

- **Engaging Stakeholders as Allies:** The Diplomat identifies key stakeholders and proactively engages them in the project from the outset. They build rapport, listen to their concerns, and address their expectations, ensuring that stakeholders feel valued and invested in the team's success. By forging strong relationships with stakeholders, the Diplomat creates a network of support that can be invaluable throughout the collaborative journey.

The Diplomat: Communicator
Step 2: Analyze – Bridging Perspectives and Building Consensus

The Diplomat ensures that diverse perspectives are heard and considered by:

- **Assessing Conflict Potential:** The Diplomat is adept at reading the emotional undercurrents within the team. They proactively identify potential sources of conflict, whether it's due to personality clashes, competing priorities, or differing opinions. By anticipating and addressing these issues early on, they prevent minor disagreements from escalating into major conflicts.

- **Facilitating Open Dialogue:** The Diplomat creates a safe space for open and honest communication. They encourage team members to share their thoughts and feelings, even if they differ from the prevailing opinion. They foster a culture of respectful disagreement, where diverse perspectives are valued and debated constructively.

- **Engaging Stakeholders in Dialogue:** The Diplomat actively seeks input from stakeholders, ensuring that their perspectives are heard and considered. They facilitate open dialogue between the team and stakeholders, addressing concerns, clarifying misunderstandings, and building consensus around the project's goals and direction.

The Diplomat: Communicator
Step 3: Develop – Nurturing Creative Collaboration

The Diplomat fosters a collaborative and creative environment by:

- **Facilitating Brainstorming with Empathy:** The Diplomat leads brainstorming sessions with empathy and understanding, ensuring that all voices are heard and all ideas are considered. They encourage the team to think outside the box, challenge assumptions, and explore unconventional approaches. Their ability to create a safe and supportive environment fosters creativity and innovation.

- **Empowering Conflict Resolution:** The Diplomat equips the team with the tools and skills needed to resolve conflicts constructively. They teach the team to focus on interests rather than positions, to seek win-win solutions, and to use conflict as an opportunity for growth and learning. By empowering the team to resolve their own conflicts, the Diplomat builds trust and resilience within the group.

- **Refining Stakeholder Communication:** The Diplomat refines the stakeholder communication plan based on the evolving needs of the project. They ensure that stakeholders are kept informed of progress, challenges, and decisions. They proactively address any concerns or objections, ensuring that stakeholders remain engaged and supportive.

The Diplomat: Communicator
Step 4: Evaluate – Navigating Decision-Making with Diplomacy

The Diplomat guides the team through the decision-making process with tact and sensitivity:

- **Mediating Conflicts and Building Consensus:** The Diplomat plays a crucial role in mediating any conflicts or disagreements that arise during the evaluation step. They facilitate open dialogue, encourage active listening, and help team members find common ground. They promote a collaborative approach to decision-making, where everyone feels heard and respected.
- **Incorporating Stakeholder Feedback:** The Diplomat gathers feedback from stakeholders on the proposed solutions, carefully considering their perspectives and concerns. They communicate the team's rationale for the chosen solution in a clear and transparent manner, addressing any objections or reservations.
- **Ensuring Buy-in and Commitment:** The Diplomat works to build consensus among team members and stakeholders, ensuring that everyone is aligned with the final decision and committed to its success. They foster a sense of shared ownership in the decision, recognizing that buy-in is essential for effective implementation.

The Diplomat sustains a positive team dynamic during implementation by:

- **Nurturing a Supportive Environment:** The Diplomat creates a culture of support and encouragement, celebrating successes and recognizing individual contributions. They provide constructive feedback, offer guidance and support, and create a safe space for team members to express their concerns or challenges.

- **Facilitating Open Communication:** The Diplomat ensures that communication channels remain open and transparent throughout the implementation step. They encourage team members to share their ideas, concerns, and feedback openly and honestly. They also maintain regular communication with stakeholders, keeping them informed of progress and addressing any concerns.

- **Building Strong Relationships:** The Diplomat continues to build and nurture relationships with stakeholders, ensuring their continued support and involvement in the project. They proactively address any issues that may arise, working collaboratively to find solutions that benefit everyone involved.

The Diplomat: Communicator
Step 6: Consolidate – Celebrating Success and Fostering Growth

The Diplomat cultivates a culture of continuous improvement by:

- **Facilitating Feedback and Reflection:** The Diplomat creates a safe and supportive environment for team members to reflect on their experiences, share feedback, and celebrate successes. They encourage open and honest dialogue, helping the team identify lessons learned and areas for improvement.
- **Documenting Lessons Learned:** The Diplomat carefully documents the team's insights and experiences, capturing lessons learned regarding communication, conflict resolution, and stakeholder engagement. This valuable knowledge is then shared with the wider organization to enhance future collaborations.
- **Celebrating Achievements:** The Diplomat recognizes and celebrates the team's accomplishments, acknowledging the contributions of each member and fostering a sense of pride and accomplishment. They create a culture of celebration, where success is recognized and appreciated, motivating the team to continue striving for excellence.

The Diplomat, with their exceptional communication skills, empathy, and ability to build bridges between people, is an indispensable asset to any team. Their presence ensures that the collaborative journey is not only productive but also harmonious, fulfilling, and ultimately successful.

6. The Cartographer: Analyst

"Facts do not cease to exist because they are ignored." – Aldous Huxley

In the age of information, where knowledge truly is power, the Cartographer emerges as the indispensable guide, transforming raw data into actionable insights. Like Charles Darwin meticulously documenting the flora and fauna of uncharted lands, or *Star Trek*'s Data, analyzing information with his positronic brain, the Cartographer is the team's seeker of truth, the master of data and information.

Their role transcends mere number-crunching; they are the navigators of the informational landscape, the interpreters of hidden truths, and the guides who help the team make informed decisions based on empirical evidence. Their analytical prowess, meticulous observation, and ability to synthesize disparate information are crucial for charting a successful course through the ever-changing seas of the business world. The Cartographer doesn't merely collect data; they transform it into a powerful tool for strategic decision-making and innovation.

At each stage of the Team Collaboration Process (TCP), the Cartographer plays a critical role in ensuring the team's decisions are grounded in reality and informed by evidence:

The Cartographer: Analyst
Step 1: Orient - Illuminating the Terrain

The Cartographer begins the journey by mapping the informational landscape:

- **Data Collection and Curation:** Like a skilled explorer gathering specimens, the Cartographer identifies and gathers relevant data sources, both internal and external, that will shed light on the project's landscape. They meticulously curate this data, ensuring its accuracy, reliability, and relevance to the team's objectives. This initial data collection provides a panoramic view of the terrain, revealing potential opportunities, challenges, and hidden patterns that can inform the team's strategic decisions. The Cartographer's expertise lies in their ability to discern what data is truly valuable, filtering out the noise and focusing on the signals that matter.

- **Preliminary Data Analysis:** With a discerning eye, the Cartographer examines the collected data, identifying key trends, patterns, or potential roadblocks. Like a seasoned geologist examining rock formations, they uncover clues that hint at the underlying structures and dynamics of the market or industry. This initial analysis provides a snapshot of the current situation and helps the team formulate initial questions and hypotheses. The Cartographer's ability to translate raw data into meaningful insights is essential for setting the stage for informed decision-making.

- **Data-Driven Insights:** The Cartographer transforms complex data into clear, concise insights that are easily understood by the team. They present their findings in a compelling and accessible manner, using charts, graphs, and visualizations to illuminate the key takeaways that will guide the team's decision-making process. The Cartographer's ability to communicate data effectively empowers the team to make informed choices and navigate the complexities of the project with confidence.

The Cartographer: Analyst
Step 2: Analyze - Charting the Depths of Information

The Cartographer dives deeper into the data, uncovering the unseen:

- **In-Depth Data Exploration:** Like a deep-sea diver venturing into the unknown, the Cartographer explores the depths of the data, using sophisticated analytical tools and techniques to uncover hidden patterns, correlations, and insights. They delve into the data's nuances, seeking to understand the underlying causes and effects that drive the team's performance and impact the market landscape. The Cartographer's relentless pursuit of knowledge and their ability to connect seemingly disparate data points can lead to breakthrough discoveries and innovative solutions.

- **Hypothesis Testing and Validation:** With a scientific mindset, the Cartographer develops and tests hypotheses based on the data. They seek to validate assumptions or uncover new information that could refine the team's understanding of the problem or opportunity at hand. This iterative process of hypothesis testing ensures that the team's decisions are based on evidence, not speculation. By rigorously testing their assumptions, the Cartographer helps the team avoid costly mistakes and make decisions based on a solid foundation of knowledge.

- **Scenario Modeling:** Using their analytical prowess, the Cartographer creates models that simulate different scenarios and explore the potential outcomes of various decisions and strategies. Like a seasoned meteorologist predicting weather patterns, they use data to forecast future trends, assess risks, and identify opportunities. This foresight enables the team to make informed choices and prepare for different contingencies, ensuring they are ready to navigate any challenges that may arise.

The Cartographer ensures that solutions are data-informed and actionable:

- **Data-Driven Decision Support:** The Cartographer acts as a trusted advisor, providing data-driven insights and recommendations to guide the team's development of solutions and strategies. They help the team prioritize ideas based on their potential impact, feasibility, and alignment with data-backed evidence. Like a seasoned pilot relying on instruments to navigate through fog, the team relies on the Cartographer's data-driven insights to make informed choices that lead to success.

- **Metric Identification and Tracking:** The Cartographer identifies and defines key performance indicators (KPIs) that will be used to measure the success of the chosen strategies and track progress towards the goals. This ensures that the team's efforts are focused on measurable outcomes and that they can objectively evaluate their performance. By establishing clear metrics, the Cartographer provides the team with a compass to guide their actions and measure their impact.

- **Data-Driven Refinement:** The Cartographer doesn't just provide initial insights; they continue to analyze data throughout the development process. They provide feedback and recommendations based on emerging trends and patterns, helping the team refine their solutions and strategies in real-time. This iterative process ensures that the team's work is constantly evolving and adapting to the changing landscape.

The Cartographer: Analyst
Step 4: Evaluate - Charting the Best Course

The Cartographer provides objective evidence for decision-making:

- **Data-Driven Evaluation:** The Cartographer meticulously evaluates potential solutions and strategies using data-driven criteria, such as cost-benefit analysis, return on investment (ROI), and risk assessment. They provide a clear, unbiased view of the potential outcomes of each option, ensuring the team's choices are grounded in solid evidence rather than gut feelings. This objective evaluation can help to mitigate biases and ensure that the team selects the most promising path forward.

- **Comparative Analysis:** The Cartographer leverages their expertise in data visualization to create compelling charts, graphs, and other visual aids that compare different options side-by-side. This allows the team to easily grasp the nuances of each choice and make informed decisions based on a clear understanding of the potential risks and rewards.

- **Validation of Assumptions:** The Cartographer rigorously tests the assumptions underlying the chosen solution using data and evidence. They challenge the team to question their beliefs and assumptions, ensuring that the final decision is based on a thorough understanding of the facts. This process of validation helps to mitigate the risk of making decisions based on faulty or incomplete information.

The Cartographer: Analyst
Step 5: Maneuver - Navigating with Real-Time Insights

The Cartographer monitors progress and provides real-time insights to determine intelligence triggers for decision points:

- **Data Collection and Monitoring:** The Cartographer establishes robust systems to collect data on the implementation of the chosen strategy. They track KPIs, monitor progress towards goals, and identify any deviations from the plan. This real-time monitoring acts as a radar, alerting the team to potential obstacles or opportunities that may arise along the way. By providing a constant stream of data-driven feedback, the Cartographer empowers the team to make informed adjustments and course corrections as needed.

- **Performance Analysis:** The Cartographer continuously analyzes the incoming data, measuring the effectiveness of the strategy and identifying areas for improvement. They provide regular reports and updates to the team, highlighting trends, patterns, and insights that can inform ongoing decision-making. Their ability to translate complex data into actionable insights empowers the team to make informed decisions and stay ahead of the curve.

- **Data-Driven Optimization:** The Cartographer doesn't just report on the data; they use it to optimize the team's strategy. Based on their analysis, they recommend adjustments and optimizations, ensuring that the team remains agile and responsive to changing circumstances. Their data-driven insights enable the team to continuously improve their approach, maximizing efficiency and effectiveness.

The Cartographer: Analyst
Step 6: Consolidate - Charting the Course for Future Success

The Cartographer ensures that the team's learning journey continues and maximizes the joy in accomplishments:

- **Post-Project Data Analysis:** After the completion of the project, the Cartographer conducts a comprehensive analysis of the data collected throughout the process. They evaluate the overall performance, identify successes and failures, and extract valuable lessons learned. This post-mortem analysis provides a comprehensive understanding of what worked well and what could be improved, laying the groundwork for future success. The Cartographer's ability to identify patterns and trends in the data allows the team to learn from their experiences and make informed decisions for future projects.

- **Data-Driven Recommendations:** The Cartographer compiles a detailed report that summarizes the project's outcomes, lessons learned, and recommendations for future projects. This report, rich with data-driven insights, serves as a valuable resource for the team and the wider organization, informing future decision-making and driving continuous improvement. By sharing their knowledge and expertise, the Cartographer ensures that the team's learning is not lost but rather becomes a catalyst for future innovation.

- **Knowledge Sharing:** The Cartographer doesn't just analyze data; they also empower the team to become more data-driven in their decision-making. They share their knowledge and expertise, teaching the team how to collect, analyze, and interpret data effectively. This creates a culture of data-driven decision-making, where everyone is empowered to use information to drive their actions and achieve their goals. By fostering a data-literate team, the Cartographer ensures that the organization's decision-making is grounded in evidence and insights, rather than gut feeling or intuition.

The Cartographer, with their unwavering commitment to data-driven insights, is a tremendous enabler for any collaborative endeavor. They illuminate the path with the light of knowledge, ensuring that the team's decisions are grounded in reality and informed by evidence. By embracing the Cartographer's analytical mindset and data-driven approach, teams can navigate the complexities of the business world with confidence, making informed choices that lead to lasting success. The Cartographer's legacy is one of clarity, insight, and informed action, leaving a trail of data-driven decisions that pave the way for future achievements.

7. The Specialist: Consultant

"The only source of knowledge is experience." – Albert Einstein

In the intricate tapestry of team collaboration, the Specialist stands as the beacon of knowledge and wisdom. Like Albert Einstein, whose profound understanding of the universe revolutionized our understanding of physics, or Spock, the Vulcan science officer whose logical insights guided the Starship *Enterprise* through countless challenges, the Specialist brings a depth of knowledge and technical mastery that is invaluable to the team. They are the subject matter experts, the seasoned professionals who have honed their skills through years of experience and dedication.

The Specialist's role extends far beyond simply providing information. They are the advisors, the problem-solvers, and the guardians of quality. Their expertise ensures that the team's work is not only innovative but also technically sound, reliable, and compliant with industry standards and regulations.

At each stage of the Team Collaboration Process (TCP), the Specialist contributes their unique expertise to ensure the team's decisions and actions are informed and effective:

The Specialist: Consultant
Step 1: Orient - Sharing the Wisdom of Experience

The Specialist sets the stage for informed decision-making:

- **Expertise Assessment:** Like a seasoned guide sharing a map of uncharted territory, the Specialist clearly communicates their area of expertise and its relevance to the project's objectives. They provide a comprehensive overview of key concepts, challenges, and opportunities in their field, ensuring the team has a solid foundation for understanding the complexities ahead.

- **Knowledge Transfer:** The Specialist generously shares their knowledge and insights, educating the team on industry trends, best practices, and potential pitfalls. They demystify jargon, translate technical concepts into layman's terms, and provide context for the team's work. This knowledge transfer empowers the team to make informed decisions and approach the project with confidence.

- **Initial Technical Feasibility Assessment:** Leveraging their experience and expertise, the Specialist provides an initial assessment of the project's technical feasibility. They identify potential constraints, risks, and limitations early on, ensuring that the team's aspirations align with reality. This early reality check helps the team avoid costly mistakes and make informed decisions about the project's scope and direction.

The Specialist: Consultant
Step 2: Analyze - Deepening the Team's Understanding

The Specialist deepens the team's understanding of the domain:

- **In-Depth Analysis:** The Specialist conducts a meticulous analysis of the project's requirements within their area of expertise. They delve into the technical details, identifying potential challenges and exploring a range of solutions based on their knowledge and experience. This in-depth analysis provides the team with a solid understanding of the technical landscape and potential obstacles, enabling them to make informed choices.

- **Expert Opinion:** The Specialist serves as a trusted advisor, offering their expert opinions and insights on technical feasibility, industry standards, regulatory compliance, and best practices. They guide the team towards the most effective approaches, tools, and technologies to achieve the project's goals. Their experience and knowledge are invaluable in navigating the complexities of the chosen domain.

- **Research and Data Collection:** The Specialist supplements the Cartographer's efforts by conducting specialized research and gathering relevant data from industry-specific sources. They leverage their network of contacts, access to specialized publications, and deep understanding of the field to provide the team with the most up-to-date and relevant information.

The Specialist: Consultant
Step 3: Develop - Crafting Solutions with Precision

The Specialist ensures the technical soundness of the team's solutions:

- **Technical Solution Design:** The Specialist actively participates in the development of solutions, contributing their expertise to ensure that the chosen approach is technically sound, feasible, and aligned with industry standards. They help to create detailed technical specifications, blueprints, and design documents that guide the implementation process. Their meticulous attention to detail ensures that the solution is not only innovative but also practical and built to last.

- **Technical Evaluation:** The Specialist rigorously evaluates the technical merits and potential drawbacks of different solutions, providing recommendations based on their expertise. They assess the scalability, sustainability, and long-term viability of each option, ensuring that the team chooses the most effective and efficient approach.

- **Risk Mitigation:** The Specialist proactively identifies and addresses potential technical risks, such as vulnerabilities, performance issues, or compliance violations. They develop mitigation strategies to minimize the impact of these risks on the project, ensuring that the team is prepared for any technical challenges that may arise.

The Specialist: Consultant
Step 4: Evaluate - The Voice of Reason

The Specialist provides a critical eye and expert guidance:

- **Expert Review:** The Specialist conducts a comprehensive review of the chosen solution, meticulously scrutinizing its technical feasibility, accuracy, and adherence to best practices. They offer constructive feedback and recommendations for improvement, ensuring that the solution is robust, reliable, and meets the highest standards of quality.

- **Technical Validation:** The Specialist validates the technical assumptions and calculations made during the development phase, ensuring that the solution is grounded in sound scientific or engineering principles. They verify the accuracy of the data, the appropriateness of the methodologies, and the feasibility of the proposed implementation.

- **Expert Consultation:** The Specialist remains available for ongoing consultation and support throughout the evaluation process. They answer questions, address concerns, and provide expert guidance to ensure that the team's decisions are informed by the latest knowledge and best practices.

The Specialist: Consultant
Step 5: Maneuver - Ensuring Technical Excellence

The Specialist ensures technical excellence in implementation:

- **Technical Oversight:** The Specialist oversees the technical implementation of the chosen solution, ensuring that it is executed correctly and effectively. They provide guidance and support to the team, troubleshooting any technical challenges that may arise. Their presence ensures that the project stays on track and that the final product or service meets the highest standards of quality.

- **Troubleshooting:** When technical issues arise, the Specialist steps in with their expertise to diagnose and resolve problems quickly and efficiently. They leverage their deep knowledge and experience to find creative solutions, minimizing downtime and ensuring the project's continued progress.

- **Quality Assurance:** The Specialist monitors the technical aspects of the project to ensure that the solution meets the established quality standards and delivers the desired results. They conduct regular tests and inspections, identify any potential issues, and take corrective action as needed. Their commitment to quality ensures that the final product or service is not only innovative but also reliable and user-friendly.

The Specialist: Consultant
Step 6: Consolidate - Sharing Knowledge & Fostering Growth

The Specialist contributes to continuous learning and development:

- **Technical Post-Mortem:** The Specialist conducts a detailed technical review of the project, analyzing the performance of the solution and identifying areas for improvement. They share their insights and lessons learned with the team, fostering a culture of continuous learning and growth.
- **Knowledge Transfer:** The Specialist actively shares their knowledge and expertise with the team, mentoring and coaching other members to enhance their technical skills. They create opportunities for learning and development, ensuring that the team's technical capabilities remain sharp and up-to-date.
- **Technical Advancement:** The Specialist remains at the forefront of their field, constantly seeking new knowledge and exploring emerging technologies. They bring these insights back to the team, encouraging them to embrace innovation and stay ahead of the curve.

The Specialist, with their deep knowledge, technical prowess, and unwavering commitment to excellence, is an invaluable expert to any team. Their expertise ensures that the team's work is not only innovative but also practical, reliable, and of the highest quality. By embracing the Specialist's wisdom and insights, teams can navigate the complexities of their industry, overcome technical challenges, and achieve extraordinary results.

Why Team Archetypes Matter within TCP

The Six Steps of Team Collaboration (TCP) is more than just a process; it's a journey of shared discovery and achievement. It's a framework that empowers teams to navigate the complexities of the modern business world with clarity, purpose, and resilience.

From the initial vision-casting of the Navigator, to the meticulous planning of the Quartermaster, the creative spark of the Alchemist, the technical expertise of the Shipwright, the diplomatic finesse of the Diplomat, the data-driven insights of the Cartographer, and the specialized knowledge of the Specialist, each archetype plays a vital role in the team's success.

The TCP is not a rigid set of rules but a flexible framework that can be adapted to the unique needs and challenges of any team. It encourages open communication, fosters collaboration, and empowers individuals to contribute their best. By embracing the TCP and recognizing the value of each team member's unique contributions, you can create a culture of high performance, high satisfaction, and lasting success.

Remember, the journey is just as important as the destination. As your team navigates the uncharted waters of the business world, embrace the challenges, celebrate the victories, and never lose sight of your shared purpose. With a clear vision, a well-defined process, and a legendary crew by your side, there's no limit to what you can achieve.

So, gather your crew, set sail, and embark on your own collaborative odyssey. The winds of change may blow, but with the TCP as your compass, you'll navigate the storms, seize opportunities, and reach the shores of triumph together.

Reflect and Embark

Which archetype resonates most with you?

Which archetype class is most prevalent on your team?

How can you leverage these archetypes to enhance

collaboration and achieve success?

Figure 7: Seven Team Archetypes

Chapter 8: The Team Leader

So, *who* and *what* is the Team Leader? Many would assume that the Navigator or positional authority is the automatic Team Leader.

Not so.

Team Leaders are those who embody the three pillars for *culture*, *purpose*, and *discipline*. In your team, you want every member to embrace their Team Leadership archetype role. No one is a bystander; and every member possesses stake and ownership in the ship's success. And this is namesake of why:

In the military, the *Team Leader* is actually the lowest non-commissioned officers' (NCO) role early in their career. They swear an oath conveying the **C**ulture, **P**urpose, and **D**iscipline of an NCO.

Their biggest priority: <u>*Soldiers*</u>.

Training, developing, caring for soldiers… that is their purpose. It creates a culture of excellence, and devoted to uphold standards and discipline. Team Leaders, although typically young and with limited experience, are entrusted with a lot of responsibility and tasks. They must be eager to learn – seeking guidance and direction from senior members. These consultations can produce outstanding results for young team leaders despite the relative experience gap. In turn, their greatest legacy is doing the same for their Soldiers who will become Team Leaders. Indeed, every Team Leader must empower the next generation of Team Leaders.

Every tasking within an organization relies on a Team Leader role to accomplish it. Being a Team Leader is an honor and privilege, and many NCOs strive to collaborate through **A**wareness, **M**eaning, **M**aneuverability, and **O**wnership. And yes, they are incredibly good at it, which is why the US military is the best in the world. Those NCOs are the "backbone of our military."

If you understand the responsibility to remain vigilantly **K**een, seizing **I**nitiative, **S**tewarding resources, and **S**ynergistically striving toward a shared vision, then you truly comprehend the role of the Team Leader. This type of leadership demands *perseverance* to embrace challenges and stay the course through adversity and wrongdoings. Relationship experts and counselors often say that "love" is choosing to care for your partner's wellbeing despite knowing their bad qualities or begotten wrongdoings. In a similar vein, team leadership is choosing to develop the team's purpose and lift up their teammates despite one's own glory, vanity, talent, and prosperity.

As renowned strategist Sun Tzu advised: "In the midst of chaos, there is also opportunity." The Team Leader embodies this wisdom, identifying potential opportunities within challenges and empowering their team to turn adversity into an advantage.

Being a Team leader also means unity coupled with diversity – not ethnic diversity, but a diversity of backgrounds, personalities, strengths, and weaknesses. There are seven identified archetypes of team members in this handbook, and each can choose to embody being a Team Leader. Each can be entrusted in their function and harmoniously synergize with other members.

Team Leadership is an idea that can permeate the team's outlook… it starts with one member, then another, until the entire team has bought into the mission. It's the outliers and toxic behaviors that can disrupt the culture, purpose, and discipline if all three are not kept sacredly.

Remember, being an effective Team Leader has nothing to do with one's rank or position within a hierarchy. For instance, there are high-ranking generals and politicians who are nightmarish in teams. On the other hand, there are small business entrepreneurs and blue-collar tradesmen who vibrantly (and almost effortlessly) attract team members because their humility and excellence shines through. Indeed, pronounced Team Leaders are evident across any strata of society.

Embracing Hope and Sacrifice

The Team Leader knows that hope and aspirations are forged in the crucible of suffering. Leaders understand that true leadership is not about self-aggrandizement but about selfless service to others. As the renowned leadership expert Simon Sinek states, "Leadership is not about being in charge. It's about taking care of those in your charge."

The Team Leader, deeply rooted in this ethos, recognizes the profound fulfillment that comes from genuine love for their team, the shared mission, and the purpose that binds them together. This love transcends mere satisfaction; it's a driving force that ignites passion, fuels resilience, and fosters an unbreakable bond among team members. In this vibrant culture of camaraderie, each individual feels valued, supported, and empowered to contribute their unique talents. The Team Leader understands that true victory is not a solitary pursuit but a symphony of collective effort, where the harmonious blend of diverse skills and perspectives creates a masterpiece of achievement.

Let me share a story that illustrates this truth: There was once a poor farmer who, despite his meager means, found immense joy and satisfaction in the simple life he shared with his family.

One day, the farmer fell gravely ill.

The village doctor, a wealthy man, came to his bedside and offered his expertise. As the doctor left the humble farmhouse, he muttered to himself, "Poor farmer, he has nothing but a life of hardship."

Meanwhile, surrounded by his loving family, the farmer smiled and declared, "I am the richest man alive! Look at all the love that surrounds me. I pity the poor doctor, for he has nothing but his wealth to keep him company."

The farmer's words echo the Team Leader's philosophy: ***True wealth lies not in material possessions or individual accolades but in the shared experiences, the bonds of trust, and the collective pursuit of a meaningful purpose.***

The Team Leader, like the farmer, finds fulfillment not in the pursuit of personal glory but in the shared joy of collaborative achievement.

Building a Legacy

The Team Leader's legacy lies in the people they've influenced. Their greatest victories and proudest moments are seeing others flourish. Team Leaders are also empathetic – they realize that they're only as strong as their weakest link...and that the team's success is a reflection of their collective effort. As the African proverb goes: "If you want to go fast, go alone. If you want to go far, go together."

The Team Leader shares in the joys and burdens of the team, finding true fulfillment in the shared hardships and accomplishments. They understand that leadership is not about social media recognition or fleeting fame, but about building lasting legacies through collaboration and teamwork. Like the legendary explorers who came before them, they strive to create a legacy that will inspire and empower future generations.

Clear and Concise Intent

The Clarity Imperative: The Team Leader's Blueprint for Purposeful Collaboration

In the dynamic landscape of modern business, where change is the only constant, and complexity is the norm, the role of the Team Leader has never been more critical. To navigate the turbulent waters of uncertainty and steer their teams towards success, leaders must demonstrate a clear and concise intent. This intent serves as the *compass* that guides the team, the *rudder* that steers them through challenges, and the *anchor* that keeps them grounded in their purpose.

Clear intent is the cornerstone of effective team leadership. It is the beacon that illuminates the path towards shared goals, the unifying force that aligns individual efforts and ignites collective passion. In the words of leadership expert John C. Maxwell: "A leader is one who knows the way, goes the way, and shows the way." This "way" is precisely what clear intent defines – a shared understanding of the team's mission, its desired outcomes, and the strategic path to achieve them.

In the absence of a clear intent, teams flounder in ambiguity, misaligned efforts, and wasted resources. A lack of clarity breeds confusion, erodes trust, and stifles creativity. Conversely, a well-defined intent empowers team members, fostering a sense of ownership and accountability. It provides a framework for decision-making, allowing the team to navigate complexities with confidence and agility.

It answers the fundamental questions that drive every successful endeavor:

- **Why:** What is the overarching purpose of our work? What impact and end-state are we striving to make?
- **What:** What are the specific, measurable goals we need to achieve? What is our decisive advantage and mission?
- **How:** What strategies and tactics will we employ to reach our objectives? What resources are required?

The Anatomy of Clear Guidance

Clear guidance comprises several key elements:

- **Vision:** A compelling vision that paints a vivid picture of the future the team is working towards. It answers the question, "What do we want to achieve?"
- **Values:** A set of shared values that guide the team's behavior and decision-making. It answers the question, "How will we conduct ourselves along the way?"
- **Goals:** Specific, measurable, achievable, relevant, and time-bound (SMART) goals that provide a roadmap for success. It answers the question, "What are the milestones we need to reach?"
- **Strategies:** The overarching approaches and tactics that will be employed to achieve the goals. It answers the question, "How will we get there?"
- **Metrics:** The key performance indicators (KPIs) that will be used to track progress and measure success. It answers the question, "How will we know we're succeeding?"

The Practical Checklist for Crafting Initiative

To craft disciplined initiative using intent and guidance, Team Leaders can follow this practical checklist:

1. **Define the "Why":** Begin by articulating the overarching purpose of the project or initiative. Why does this work matter? What impact will it have on the organization, customers, or society?
2. **Set SMART Goals:** Break down the overarching vision into specific, measurable, achievable, relevant, and time-bound goals. This provides a tangible roadmap for success and allows for progress tracking.
3. **Identify Key Strategies:** Determine the overarching approaches and tactics that will be employed to achieve the goals. Consider different options, weigh their pros and cons, and select the most viable

strategies.

4. **Allocate Resources:** Identify the resources (time, budget, personnel) required to implement the strategies and achieve the goals. Ensure that resources are allocated effectively and efficiently.

5. **Establish Metrics:** Define the key performance indicators (KPIs) that will be used to measure progress and evaluate success. These metrics should be aligned with the overall goals and provide actionable insights.

6. **Communicate Clearly:** Share the intent with the team in a clear, concise, and compelling manner. Ensure that everyone understands the vision, values, goals, strategies, and metrics.

7. **Foster Collaboration:** Encourage open communication and collaboration among team members. Invite feedback, questions, and suggestions to ensure that everyone feels heard and involved.

8. **Adapt and Iterate:** The business landscape is constantly evolving. Be prepared to adapt and iterate the intent as needed based on new information, feedback, and changing circumstances.

Team Leaders' Role: Beyond Decision-Making

While the Team Leaders are ultimately responsible for making decisions in their role, it extends far beyond simply barking demands and orders. They are the architects of the team's culture, the facilitators of collaboration, and the champions of their members' growth and development.

The Team Leader must lead by example, embodying the values and behaviors they expect from their team. They must foster a culture of trust, respect, and open communication, where everyone feels valued and empowered to contribute their best. They must also be willing to listen, learn, and adapt, recognizing that the best ideas often come from unexpected sources.

As leadership expert Stephen Covey wrote: "Effective leadership is putting first things first. Effective management is discipline, carrying it out." The Team Leader must not only prioritize the right things but also ensure that the team is disciplined in executing their plans.

By crafting a clear and concise intent and leading by example, the Team Leader lays the groundwork for a collaborative odyssey. They empower their team to navigate the complexities of the business world, overcome challenges, seize opportunities, and ultimately achieve shared success.

Chapter 9:
Two Distinct Outcomes

Realizing High Performance

The pursuit of high performance is a constant in the business world. Companies strive for it, teams are measured by it, and individuals are often rewarded based on their ability to achieve it. But what does high performance truly mean, and how is it achieved within the context of team collaboration?

High performance, in its simplest form, is the ability to consistently exceed expectations and deliver exceptional results. It's about going above and beyond the ordinary, pushing boundaries, and achieving remarkable outcomes. In the context of team collaboration, high performance is the result of a synergistic effort, where the whole is greater than the sum of its parts.

The Team Collaboration Process (TCP) is designed to facilitate this synergy, enabling teams to achieve high performance through a structured and collaborative approach. By following the six steps of TCP - Orient, Analyze, Develop, Evaluate, Maneuver, and Consolidate – teams can harness their collective intelligence, creativity, and expertise to achieve extraordinary results.

However, high performance is not solely about achieving objectives. It's also about creating a sustainable and fulfilling work environment, where team members feel valued, empowered, and motivated to contribute their best. This is where the second outcome, high satisfaction, comes into play.

Realizing High Satisfaction

High satisfaction is the emotional counterpart to high performance. It's the feeling of fulfillment, engagement, and enjoyment that comes from doing meaningful work with a team you respect and admire. When team members are satisfied with their work, they are more likely to be motivated, productive, and loyal to the organization.

The TCP is designed to foster high satisfaction by promoting collaboration, communication, and a sense of shared purpose. By working together towards a common goal, team members build strong relationships, develop their skills, and contribute to something larger than themselves. This sense of belonging and purpose is a key driver of job satisfaction.

Moreover, the TCP emphasizes continuous learning and improvement, providing opportunities for team members to grow and develop both personally and professionally. This ongoing development not only enhances individual performance but also contributes to a sense of fulfillment and satisfaction.

Three Avenues of Fulfillment

To create a high-performing and highly satisfied team, leaders must focus on three key avenues for fulfillment:

1. **Works of Faith:** Encourage team members to believe in the mission, the team, and themselves. This faith fuels resilience, perseverance, and a willingness to take risks. When team members have faith in their mission, they are more likely to stay committed during challenging times, knowing that their efforts contribute to a greater purpose. This belief in the mission and in each other creates a strong foundation of trust and unity, enabling the team to tackle obstacles with confidence and determination.

2.   **Labors of Love:** Foster a culture of perseverance, diligence, and passion for their work. When team members love what they do and whom they do it with, they are more likely to go above and beyond, to innovate, and to create exceptional results. Passionate team members are driven by intrinsic motivation, finding joy and satisfaction in their daily tasks. This culture of love for the work and for the team fosters a positive and energetic environment, where creativity and collaboration thrive. It also encourages team members to support one another, creating a sense of camaraderie and shared purpose.

3.   **Steadfastness of Hope:** hope for the future, both for the team and for each individual. This hope provides a sense of purpose and direction, motivating team members to overcome challenges and strive for continuous improvement. Hope acts as a guiding light, helping team members to see beyond immediate difficulties and focus on long-term goals. By instilling hope, leaders can help their team maintain a positive outlook, even in the face of adversity. This sense of hope encourages resilience and adaptability, enabling the team to navigate change and uncertainty with confidence.

By nurturing these three avenues, leaders can create a team environment where both high performance and high satisfaction are not only achievable but sustainable. As iron sharpens iron, so too does a collaborative team sharpen each member, fostering growth, development, and a deep sense of fulfillment. The journey towards these outcomes is not always easy, but the rewards are immeasurable. A high-performing, highly satisfied team is a force to be reckoned with, capable of achieving extraordinary results and leaving a lasting legacy.

Chapter 10:
Applying the "So What"

Cultivating the Grounds

The principles and archetypes explored in this book offer a compelling framework for team collaboration, but the question remains: How do we translate these concepts into tangible results in our unique organizational contexts? The "so what" is about bridging the gap between theory and practice, understanding how to cultivate high-performing teams regardless of the challenges and constraints we face.

Adapting to Diverse Landscapes

Every organization is a unique ecosystem, with its own culture, values, and operational realities. Whether it's a Fortune 500 corporation, a small startup, a government agency, or a community organization, the principles of collaboration remain the same. However, the implementation may vary depending on the specific context.

In the military, for instance, teams are often built from scratch, with members hailing from diverse backgrounds and experiences. The emphasis on discipline, hierarchy, and adherence to standard operating procedures creates a unique environment for collaboration. In contrast, a tech startup might have a flatter organizational structure, with a focus on agility, innovation, and individual autonomy.

Despite these differences, the core principles of TCP can be adapted to any environment. The key is to identify the specific challenges and opportunities within your organization and tailor your approach accordingly.

Catalysts and Hindrances to Team Cohesion

Let's examine some common catalysts and hindrances to team cohesion, drawing inspiration from diverse organizational models:

- **Solely Focusing on Your Job:** In highly specialized fields like Special Forces, individuals are often laser-focused on their specific roles, with limited exposure to other aspects of the operation. While this specialization can be a strength, it can also hinder collaboration if not balanced with cross-training and a broader understanding of the team's mission.

- **Picking and Choosing Your Team:** In some organizations, like Special Forces, team members are carefully selected based on their skills and compatibility. This can create a strong sense of cohesion, but it's not always feasible in environments like the military or the Church, where teams are often formed based on necessity rather than choice.

- **Additional Details and Responsibilities:** Organizations like the military often have a multitude of "additional details" – tasks and responsibilities that fall outside of core job functions. These details can create distractions and hinder focus on the primary mission.

Building High-Performing Teams in Any Environment

So, how can we build high-performing teams in environments that don't allow for hand-picked members or a singular focus on core responsibilities?

1. **Foster a Culture of Shared Purpose:** Regardless of the organizational structure, creating a strong sense of shared purpose is essential. This involves clearly communicating the team's mission, values, and goals, and ensuring that everyone understands how their individual contributions fit into the bigger picture.

2. **Embrace Diversity:** Diversity of thought, experience, and background can be a powerful asset for any team.

Encourage open communication and respect for different perspectives, and leverage the unique strengths of each team member to achieve common goals.

3. **Encourage Cross-Training and Development:** Provide opportunities for team members to learn new skills and gain a broader understanding of the team's mission. This can foster empathy, increase flexibility, and enhance problem-solving capabilities.

4. **Streamline Processes and Prioritize Tasks:** Identify and eliminate unnecessary "additional details" that can distract from the team's core mission. Focus on prioritizing essential tasks and streamlining processes to maximize efficiency and effectiveness.

5. **Celebrate Collective Achievement:** Recognize and reward team achievements rather than solely focusing on individual contributions. This fosters a sense of shared responsibility and reinforces the importance of collaboration.

The "So What": Your Team's Transformative Journey

The "so what" of the Team Leadership Philosophy lies in its profound ability to transform any group of individuals into a high-performing team. By embracing the archetypal roles, fostering a culture of collaboration, and adapting the process to your unique organizational context, you can unleash the full potential of your team. This transformation is not just about achieving productivity; it's about creating a deeply satisfying and fulfilling experience for every team member.

Whether you're leading a military unit, a business startup, or a corporate team, the Team Leadership Handbook can help you build a team that is not only productive but also deeply satisfying. The journey may be challenging, but the rewards are immeasurable. As you embark on this collaborative odyssey, remember that the true power of your team lies not in individual brilliance, but in the collective wisdom, creativity, and resilience that emerges when diverse talents unite in the pursuit of a shared goal.

The TCP is more than a methodology; it's rooted in a philosophy that emphasizes the importance of each team member's unique contributions. By recognizing and leveraging the strengths of each archetype, you create a dynamic synergy that drives innovation and excellence. The Navigator's strategic vision, the Quartermaster's meticulous planning, the Alchemist's boundless creativity, the Shipwright's technical expertise, the Diplomat's empathetic communication, the Cartographer's analytical insights, and the Specialist's deep knowledge all come together to form a cohesive and unstoppable force.

As you implement the Team Leadership Model, you'll witness the transformation of your team from a collection of individuals into a harmonious and high-performing unit. This process fosters a sense of belonging and purpose, where each member feels valued and empowered to contribute their best. The collaborative environment nurtures trust, respect, and mutual support, creating a positive and motivating atmosphere that drives continuous improvement and growth.

The journey towards these outcomes is not always easy, but the rewards are immeasurable. A high-performing, highly satisfied team is a force to be reckoned with, capable of achieving extraordinary results and leaving a lasting legacy. By embracing being a Team Leader, you are not only enhancing your team's performance but also enriching the lives of its members, fostering a culture of excellence, and creating a lasting impact on your organization and beyond.

Appendix A:
Interrogative Questions

In the intricate dance of leadership, it's easy to fall into the trap of assuming that your role is primarily to provide answers. However, the most impactful leaders often discover that the true art of leadership lies in asking the right questions. Interrogative questions – those that seek information and encourage reflection – are a powerful tool for unlocking the hidden potential within your team, fostering deeper understanding, and propelling your collective efforts towards extraordinary outcomes.

Think of it like this: Imagine you're a detective investigating a complex case. Would you rely solely on your own deductions, or would you seek the perspectives of witnesses, experts, and even suspects? The same principle applies to leadership. By asking thoughtful questions, you open up a dialogue that invites diverse viewpoints, challenges assumptions, and sparks creativity.

Consider the alternative: A leader who dictates solutions without seeking input may achieve short-term compliance, but they risk stifling innovation and eroding trust. In contrast, a leader who genuinely seeks to understand their team's perspectives and ideas cultivates an environment of collaboration, empowerment, and continuous improvement.

Let's delve into some concrete examples of how interrogative questions can transform your leadership approach:

Instead of saying: "We need to increase sales by 10% this quarter."

Ask: "What strategies do you think would be most effective in achieving our sales goals?" This question invites the team to brainstorm ideas, share their expertise, and take ownership of the solution.

Instead of saying: "This project is behind schedule. We need to work harder."

Ask: "What obstacles are we facing, and what can we do to get back on track?" This question shifts the focus from blame to problem-solving, empowering the team to identify and address the root causes of the delay.

Instead of saying: "This idea won't work."

Ask: "What are the potential risks and challenges associated with this idea, and how can we mitigate them?" This question encourages critical thinking and a thorough evaluation of the idea, rather than a knee-jerk rejection. Ultimately, the proposed idea may not work, but it warrants a thoughtful evaluation nonetheless.

Transforming Conversations with Interrogative Questions

Consider the difference between these two approaches:

- **Directive Statement:** "We need to increase our sales by 15% this quarter. Here's the marketing plan I've developed. Let's get started."

- **Interrogative Questioning:** "What are your thoughts on how we can achieve a 15% increase in sales this quarter? What unique strategies or tactics could we employ? What potential obstacles do you foresee, and how can we proactively address them?"

The first approach, while direct and efficient, limits the team's input and may stifle creativity. The second approach, however, invites collaboration, encourages diverse perspectives, and fosters a sense of shared ownership in the solution. By asking questions, you tap into the collective wisdom of your team, empowering them to contribute their unique insights and ideas.

The Art of Asking Effective Questions

To harness the power of inquiry, consider these key principles:

- **Open-Ended Questions:** Avoid yes-or-no questions that limit responses. Instead, ask open-ended questions that encourage thoughtful responses and exploration of possibilities. For example, instead of asking, "Do you think this is a good idea?", ask, "What are the potential benefits and drawbacks of this approach?"

- **Probing Questions:** Delve deeper into responses by asking follow-up questions that clarify, expand, or challenge initial thoughts. For example, if a team member suggests a new marketing strategy, you could ask, "How would this strategy differentiate us from our competitors?" or "What metrics would you use to measure the success of this approach?"

- **Empowering Questions:** Ask questions that empower team members to take ownership of their ideas and contributions. For instance, instead of asking, "How can I help you with this task?", ask, "What resources or support do you need to accomplish this goal?"

The Ripple Effect of Inquiry

The impact of interrogative questions extends far beyond the immediate conversation. When leaders consistently employ this approach, they cultivate a culture of curiosity, critical thinking, and continuous learning. They create an environment where team members feel empowered to ask questions, challenge assumptions, and explore new ideas.

This culture of inquiry not only fuels innovation but also strengthens relationships within the team. By demonstrating a genuine interest in their perspectives and ideas, leaders build trust and rapport with their team members. This, in turn, fosters a more collaborative and supportive environment where everyone feels valued and heard.

Mastery in the Power of Questions

The power of inquiry is a transformative force in leadership. By asking the right questions, you can unlock the hidden potential of your team, foster deeper understanding, and drive your organization towards unprecedented success. So, the next time you find yourself tempted to give a directive, pause and consider: What question could you ask instead? The answers you uncover may surprise and inspire you.

Appendix B:
Cheat Sheet

Culture

- **Mutual Respect:** *How can we foster an environment where every team member feels genuinely valued and respected, regardless of their role or background?*
- **Mutual Respect:** *What specific actions can we take to ensure that our team's values of dignity, trust, and integrity are upheld daily?*
- **Mutual Respect:** *How can we create opportunities for meaningful dialogue and connection that goes beyond superficial interactions?*
- **Interdependence:** *How can we design our team structure and processes to emphasize interdependence, where each member's contributions are essential to the overall success?*
- **Interdependence:** *What systems or tools can we implement to ensure transparent communication and create a shared sense of responsibility?*
- **Competition:** *How can we cultivate a healthy sense of competition within our team that drives excellence without fostering a toxic or cutthroat environment?*
- **Competition:** *What are the external threats or challenges that could undermine our team's culture, and how can we proactively address them?*
- **Excellence:** *How can we create a learning environment that encourages continuous improvement and challenges team members to reach their full potential?*
- **Excellence:** *What specific metrics or benchmarks can we use to measure our team's progress towards excellence, and how can we regularly assess and celebrate our achievements?*
- **Holistic Development:** *How can we integrate the principles of mutual respect, interdependence, and competition to create a holistic culture that fosters both individual and collective growth?*

Comprehending Purpose

- **Vision:** *What is the overarching vision that unites our team? How does our work contribute to a larger goal or impact?*
- **Vision:** *How can we articulate our shared vision in a way that inspires and motivates every team member?*
- **Vision:** *What are the potential obstacles or challenges that could hinder us from achieving our vision, and how can we proactively address them?*
- **Initiative:** *How can we foster a culture where every team member feels empowered to take initiative, propose solutions, and drive projects forward?*
- **Initiative:** *What mechanisms or processes can we implement to encourage proactive problem-solving and continuous improvement within our team?*
- **Initiative:** *How can we celebrate and reward individual initiative while still maintaining a collaborative and supportive team environment?*
- **Reinforcement:** *How can we effectively recognize and reward not only the final outcomes but also the small wins and incremental achievements along the way?*
- **Reinforcement:** *What are the most meaningful forms of recognition and reward for our team members, both individually and collectively?*
- **Reinforcement:** *How can we ensure that our reinforcement strategies align with our team's values and contribute to a positive and motivating culture?*
- **Holistic Purpose:** *How can we integrate our shared vision, individual initiative, and effective reinforcement to create a holistic sense of purpose that drives our team towards sustained success and fulfillment?*

Comprehending Discipline

- **_Goal Prioritization:_** _How do we ensure our team's focus remains on the most critical goals, especially when faced with competing priorities or distractions?_
- **_Goal Prioritization:_** _What systems or frameworks can we implement to track our progress towards these goals and adjust our strategies as needed?_
- **_Goal Prioritization:_** _How can we foster a culture of work-life balance within our team, recognizing that individual well-being is essential for sustained high performance?_
- **_Communication:_** _How can we create a communicative environment where all team members feel safe to express their ideas, concerns, and feedback openly and honestly?_
- **_Communication:_** _What communication channels or tools can we utilize to ensure that information flows freely and efficiently within the team?_
- **_Communication:_** _How can we develop our interpersonal tact and communication skills to inspire collaboration and effectively address conflict when it arises?_
- **_Conflict Resolution:_** _How can we equip our team with the skills and strategies to navigate conflict constructively, turning disagreements into opportunities for growth and innovation?_
- **_Conflict Resolution:_** _What role does empathy and understanding play in resolving conflicts within our team, and how can we foster these qualities in our interactions?_
- **_Conflict Resolution:_** _How can we create a safe space for team members to voice concerns and disagreements without fear of retribution or judgment?_
- **_Holistic Discipline:_** _How can we integrate goal prioritization, effective communication, and conflict resolution to create a disciplined team culture that thrives on collaboration, innovation, and continuous improvement?_

Practicing Awareness

- *What specific benefits* can you expect to experience by integrating mindfulness into my daily interactions with colleagues and clients, such as improved communication, reduced stress, and enhanced empathy?

- *What are some innovative and engaging ways* that incorporate mindfulness into team celebrations and recognition events, promoting a sense of gratitude, appreciation, and community among team members?

- *How can you identify and manage* internal prejudices and assumptions, specifically regarding race, gender, and socioeconomic background, to enhance my perception and avoid making biased judgments?

- *What are some common obstacles* you might face while practicing mindfulness at work, such as distractions, time constraints, or resistance from colleagues, and how can I overcome them effectively?

- *How can you cultivate* self-awareness and emotional intelligence, particularly in challenging situations, to make wiser decisions and build stronger relationships?

- *What specific strategies can you employ* to utilize mindfulness to promote creativity and innovation within my team, such as brainstorming sessions, idea generation exercises, and visualization techniques?

- *How can you gain a deeper understanding of my team members' perspectives and requirements*, fostering empathy and building a more cohesive team dynamic?

- *What practical steps can you take to establish a team environment* that is more inclusive and equitable, ensuring that all members feel valued and respected, through the practice of mindfulness?

- *How does awareness contribute to establishing trust and psychological safety* within a team, and what specific behaviors can I adopt to create a supportive and open environment?

- *How can you identify and address team dynamics* that may be obstructing cooperation and productivity, such as unresolved conflicts, power imbalances, or communication breakdowns?

Practicing Meaning

- *What are some effective ways for teams to create a safe and supportive environment* where members feel comfortable sharing their perspectives and vulnerabilities?

- *How can team leaders help individual members discover and articulate their personal values* and aspirations in relation to the team's goals?

- *What specific activities or exercises* can teams engage in to foster a shared sense of purpose and direction?

- *How can teams practically apply the concept of meaning-making* to their everyday work and interactions?

- *How can teams leverage their unique strengths and diversity* to collectively generate meaningful and impactful outcomes?

- *What strategies can teams employ to ensure that their practices and decisions* align with their core values and beliefs?

- *How can teams develop a shared language and understanding* of what constitutes "meaningful work" in their specific context?

- *What tools or resources are available to help teams measure and track* their progress in cultivating a meaningful team culture?

- *How can teams create opportunities for reflection and learning* from past experiences to inform their future practices?

- *What are some indicators or observable behaviors* that suggest a team is successfully practicing meaning and experiencing increased levels of engagement and motivation?

Practicing Maneuverability

- *Adaptability and Flexibility: How can teams cultivate a culture of agility and resilience* to navigate unexpected changes and challenges?

- *Risk Assessment: What strategies can teams use to anticipate and mitigate potential risks* associated with new initiatives or approaches?

- *Experimentation and Learning: How can teams create a safe and supportive environment* for experimentation and continuous learning from failures?

- *Cross-Functional Collaboration: What are the key challenges and opportunities of cross-functional* collaboration, and how can teams effectively leverage it to improve agility?

- *Decision-Making: How can teams decentralize decision-making* while maintaining alignment with overall strategic goals and objectives?

- *Speed and Efficiency: What are some practical techniques for streamlining processes* and improving efficiency without sacrificing quality or innovation?

- *Continuous Improvement: How can teams establish a culture of continuous improvement* and identify opportunities for optimization in their workflows?

- *Resilience and Grit: What strategies can teams use to build resilience and grit,* enabling them to bounce back from setbacks and challenges with renewed determination?

- *Technology Adoption: How can teams effectively adopt new technologies and tools* to enhance their agility and efficiency while minimizing disruption and resistance?

- *External Trends: How can teams stay informed about industry trends and emerging technologies* to anticipate and adapt to changes in their operating environment?

Practicing Ownership

- *Empowerment and Accountability: How can leaders effectively empower* team members while maintaining accountability for their results?

- *Autonomy and Control: What is the right balance between autonomy and control* for effective team collaboration, and how can leaders strike this balance?

- *Recognition and Rewards: How can recognition and rewards be used to reinforce ownership* and motivate team members to take initiative and exceed expectations?

- *Conflict Resolution: How can teams address conflicts and disagreements* in a constructive and collaborative manner that reinforces ownership and accountability?

- *Mentorship and Coaching: How can leaders provide mentorship and coaching* to help team members develop their skills and take on greater ownership of their work?

- *Performance Management: What are effective performance management strategies* for reinforcing ownership and accountability, and how can they be tailored to individual team members?

- *Failure and Learning: How can teams create a safe and supportive environment* for learning from failures and using them as opportunities for growth and development?

- *Employee Engagement: How can teams foster employee engagement and motivation* by empowering individuals to take ownership of their work?

- *Organizational Culture: How can organizations cultivate a culture of ownership* and empowerment that supports team collaboration and high performance?

Notes

Bass, B. M., & Riggio, R. E. (2006). Transformational leadership. Psychology press.

Blocker, Chris P., et al. "Scarcity as Strategy." *California Management Review*, 23 Oct. 2023.

Camm, T. W. (2019). The dark side of servant leadership.

Camp, J. (2002). Start with no: The negotiating tools that the pros don't want you to know. Currency.

Drucker, P. F. (2018). The effective executive. Routledge.

Feifer, Jason. "6 Giant Companies That Nearly Flopped." *Entrepreneur*, 1 Dec. 2020.

George, J. M. 2000. Emotions and leadership: The role of emotional intelligence. Human Relations, 53: 1027-1055.

Hoch, J. E., Bommer, W. H., Dulebohn, J. H., & Wu, D. (2018). Do ethical, authentic, and servant leadership explain variance above and beyond transformational leadership? A meta-analysis. Journal of management, 44(2), 501-529.

Jung, C. G. (1966). Collected works: the archetypes and the collective unconscious. Pantheon Books.

Kouzes, J. M., & Posner, B. Z. (2006). The leadership challenge (Vol. 3). John Wiley & Sons.

McClelland, D. C., & Burnham, D. H. 1976. Power is the great motivator. Harvard Business Review, 54: 100-110.

McCullough, M. E., Hoyt, W. T., & Rachal, K. C. (2000). What we know (and need to know) about assessing forgiveness constructs.

Lencioni, P. M. (2012). The five dysfunctions of a team: Team assessment. John Wiley & Sons.

Linden, R. M. (2010). Leading across boundaries: Creating collaborative agencies in a networked world. John Wiley & Sons.

Owolabi, D. (2020). Authentic leadership: How to lead with nothing to hide, nothing to prove & nothing to lose.

Page, D., & Wong, T. P. (2000). A conceptual framework for measuring servant leadership. *The human factor in shaping the course of history and development, 69,* 110.

Prados, J. (2015). *The US special forces: What everyone needs to know.* What Everyone Needs to Know (r).

Moore, H. G., & Guardia, M. (2018). Hal Moore on leadership. Blackstone Audio.

McChrystal, G. S., Collins, T., Silverman, D., & Fussell, C. (2015). Team of teams: new rules of engagement for a complex world. Penguin.

Sinek, S. (2009). Start with why: How great leaders inspire everyone to take action. Penguin.

Sun, T. (1994). *The art of war* (Vol. 68). Westview Press.

Vittorio, S. (2020). The Journey to Success. In *Building Your Best Chemistry Career Volume 1: Academic Perspectives* (pp. 27-33). American Chemical Society.

Dedication

This work stands as a testament not to my individual effort, but to the collective strength and unwavering support of those who have walked beside me. I am profoundly grateful.

First, to God, the source of all strength and wisdom, I am humbled amidst your faithful love and sanctification. Your grace has brought me through every challenge and blessing.

To my steadfast partner, Caroline Ann, your unwavering support as my sounding board and fortifier has been my greatest asset. To my children, your lively and often sporty dynamics and love has refined me to greater richer depths. To my parents, your enduring love and generosity has shaped my core values and rooted me in truth. To my in-laws, your deep fellowship have sharpened and grown me significantly. To my brothers and sister, our relationship has been a wealth of wisdom and joyous fellowship.

To the mentors who shared their insights, and to the NCOs, Officers, and Commanders who modeled effective leadership, I am profoundly indebted. Your examples have been invaluable. To my peers, your collaborative spirit has been an extraordinary learning adventure. To my subordinates, your trust and dedication… and often candid feedback have been the greatest honor; you are the true architects of our achievements. To the aspirational leaders whose actions and works that have inspired me, thank you!

To the teachers who instilled the value of lifelong learning, your impact is immeasurable. And to my friends, your unwavering support and shared laughter have been a constant source of strength.

This handbook is a reflection of the lessons learned through collaborative effort and the belief that strong teams can achieve extraordinary results. It is my sincere hope that it empowers leaders to build cohesive teams, foster a culture of community, and gloriously navigate challenges. I am confident that by embracing Team Leadership, we can collectively achieve our shared mission with humility, gratitude, and undeterred strength.